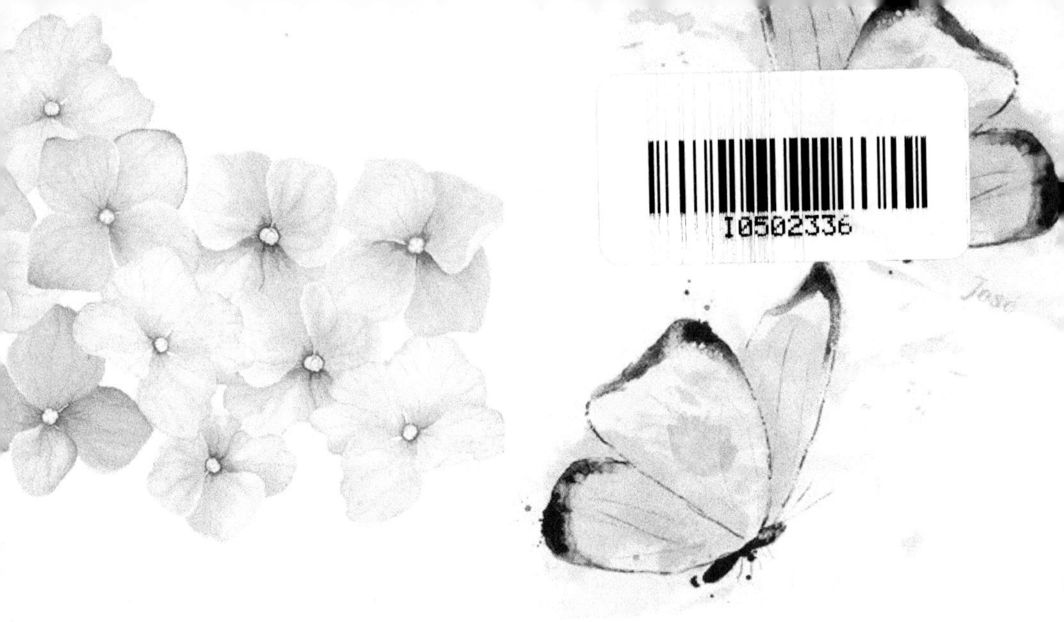

Fearless watercolor for beginners

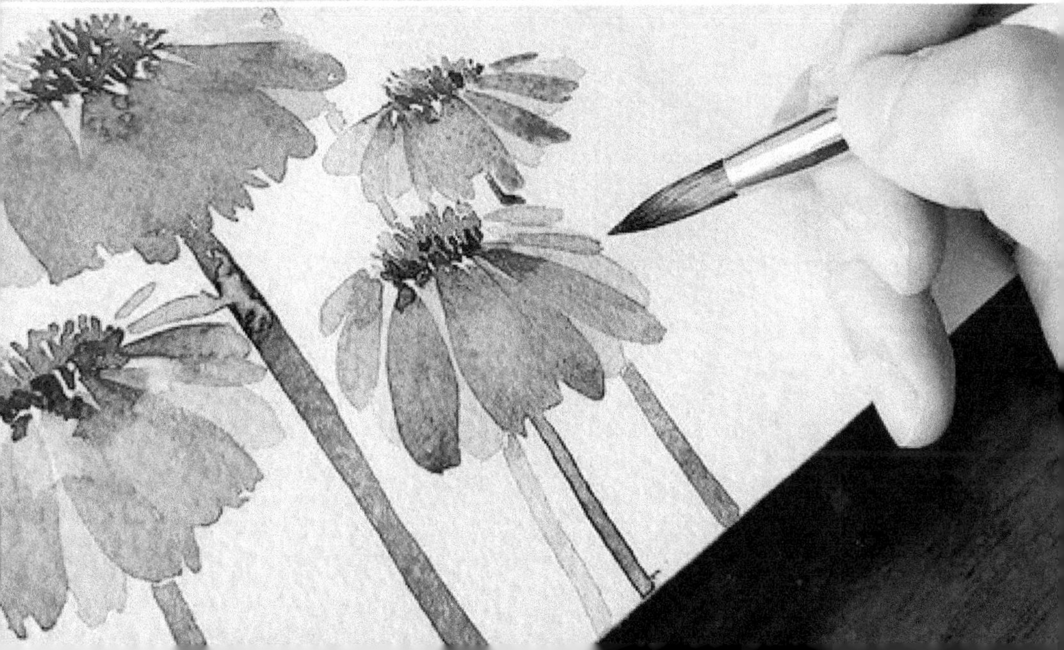

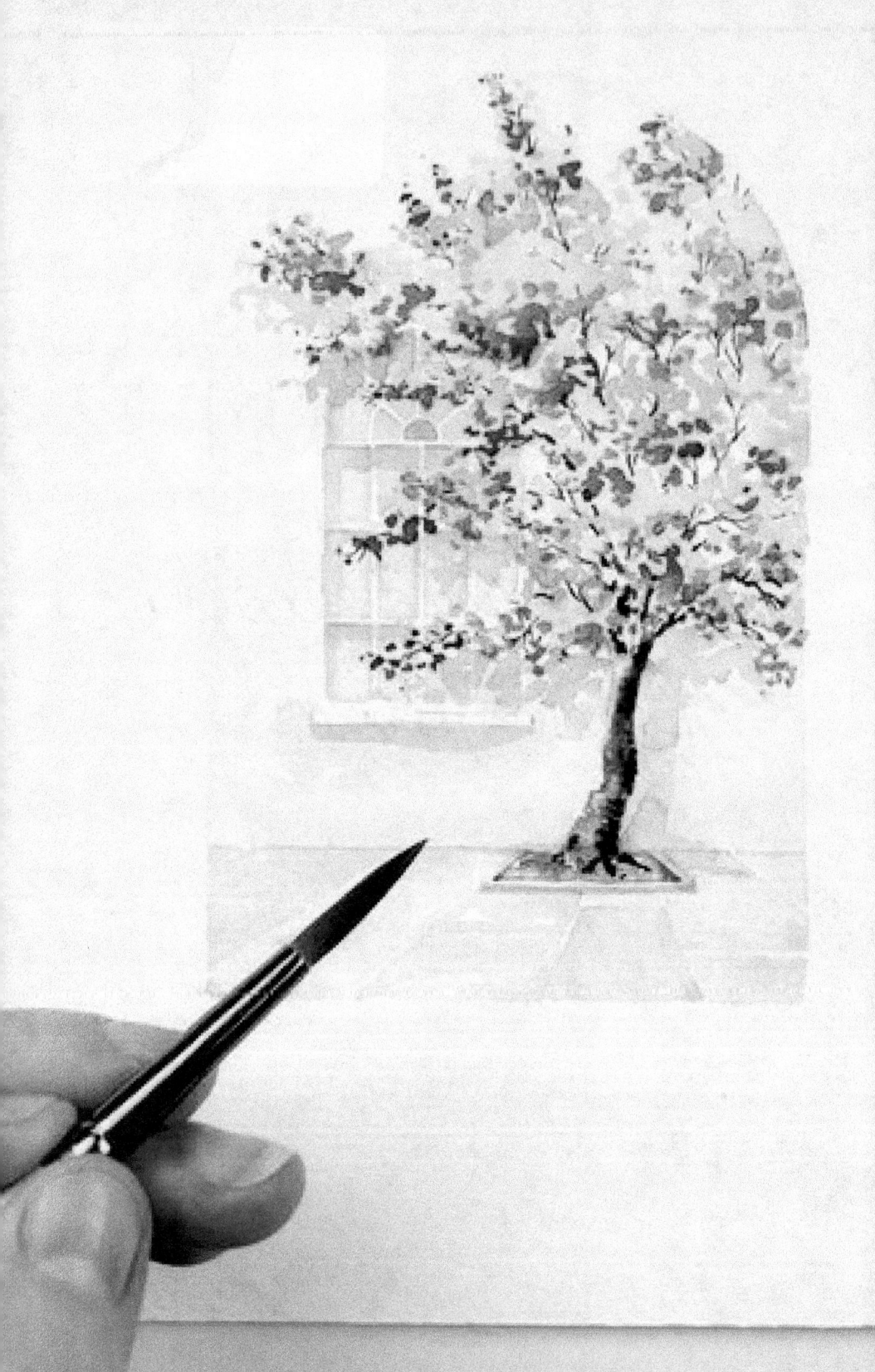

TABLE CONTENT

INTRODUCTION	1
How to Start Watercolor	3
Start Learning	5
What you need to Start	9
What to paint	12
Watercolor palette colors	23
Beginners Step by Step Tutorial	
Watercolor Still Life	34
Watercolor Coffee Painting	45
Paint Watercolor Roses	59

INTRODUCTION

Dive into Watercolor with a Splash of Fearlessness!
Have you ever been captivated by the magic of watercolor paintings? The way light dances on translucent washes, the effortless blends, the unexpected blooms of color? But maybe you hesitated to pick up a brush, fearing mistakes or a lack of artistic talent.

Fearless Watercolor for Beginners is your invitation to a world of vibrant creativity, where experimentation reigns and happy accidents become beautiful surprises. This book is not about achieving perfection, but about embracing the joyful journey of watercolor exploration. Within these pages, you'll discover:

- Essential techniques for beginners, from washes and layering to creating textures and playful effects.
- Simple step-by-step demonstrations to build your confidence and inspire you to create your own masterpieces.
- Encouragement to let go of inhibitions and explore the unique character of watercolors.

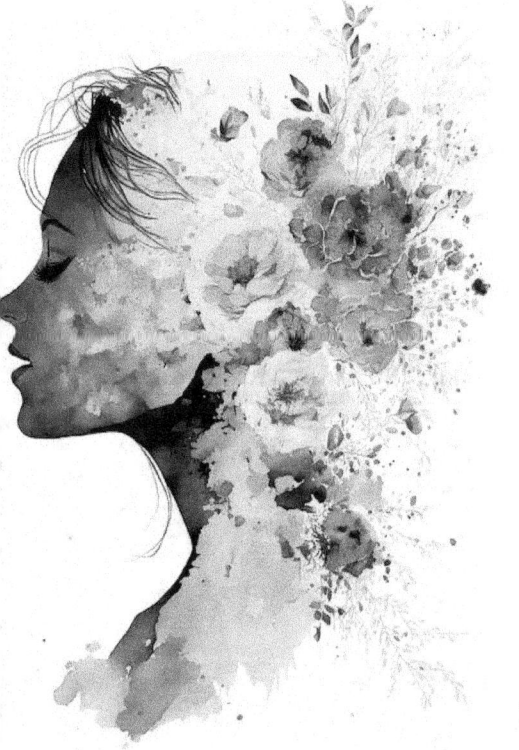

We'll venture beyond the basics, delving into creative exercises and mixed-media techniques to take your art to exciting new places. Whether you dream of painting landscapes, florals, or something entirely abstract, Fearless Watercolor for Beginners will equip you with the skills and mindset to embark on a vibrant artistic adventure. So, grab your brushes, unleash your inner artist, and get ready to paint with fearless joy!

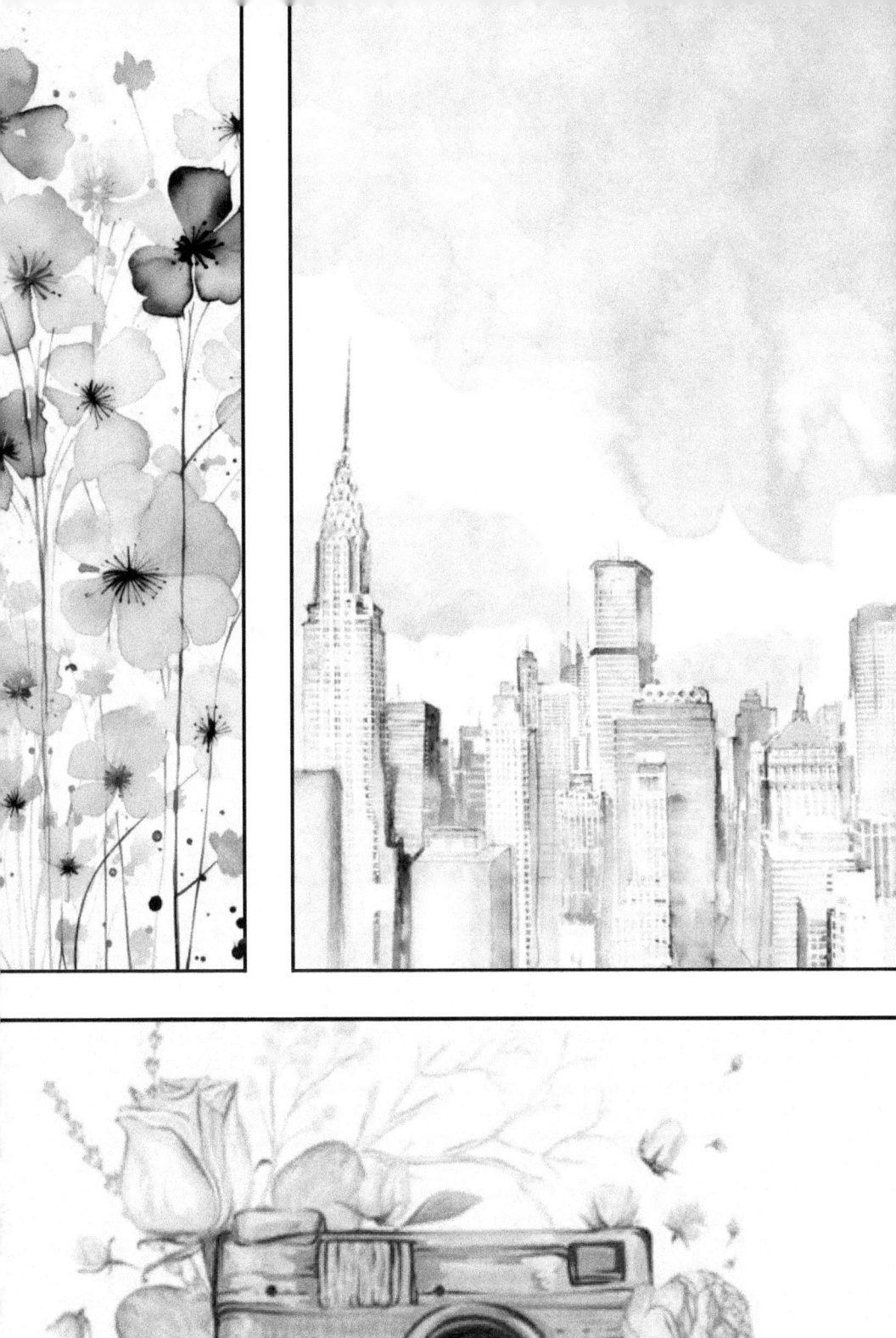

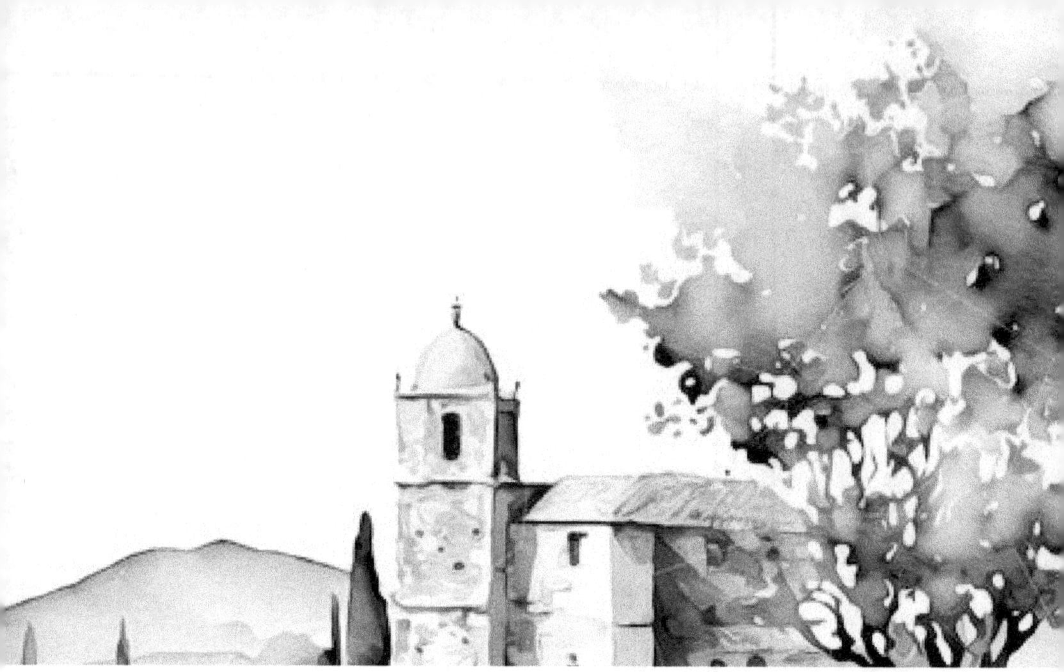

How to Start Watercolor Painting
First Steps for Beginners

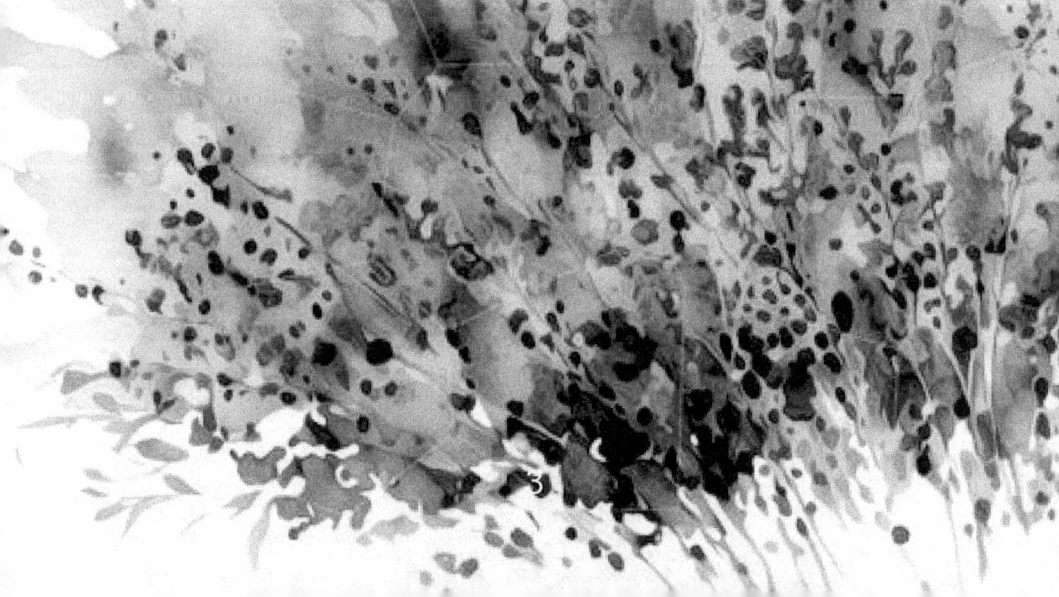

Have you ever seen a beautiful piece of watercolor art and thought "I want to paint like that"? Many budding artists hold back because they just don't know how to start painting in watercolors. I think that's too bad. Because I believe the joy of creating with watercolors is within anybody's reach. Some people simply don't know where to begin. Others have fears and frustrations that prevent them from taking the leap.

My first steps in watercolor were far from perfect. I used to be very self conscious about my artwork and I was reticent to show people the results of my paintings. I would spend forever remaking a piece of art. Heck… Even today I sometimes have to start over a few times before I'm happy with my results. But the joy of painting in watercolor keeps you coming back again and again.

I'd like to help you overcome the reasons that are holding you back, and discover the first steps you need to get started with this wonderful art medium.

Watercolor painting is one of the most rewarding and approachable forms of art. Let's examine a few simple ideas and projects to get you going on your creative journey.

How to Start Learning Watercolor Painting

There are lots of reasons why we have difficulty starting something new like watercolor painting. Maybe you don't understand how to use watercolors to get the best out of them. Or you don't know which supplies to buy. Some people are worried about not doing the right things when they paint, and wonder what to practice in order to make progress? And then you have to find the time and the motivation to actually paint.

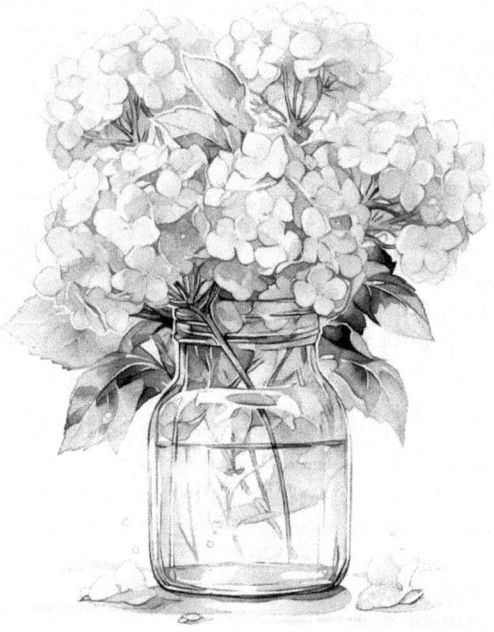

If you let any of these things prevent you from starting watercolors then you are quite simply missing out on one of the most satisfying and beautiful art practices around. But it's not difficult to get over these obstacles

Lack of confidence

Fear of the unknown is a natural human response to anything new. You're not alone and it's not unusual. I wasn't 100% confident in my painting abilities when I first started. But as soon as you get over that fear you wonder what was preventing you! Watercolor painting is the same. "But what if I make a mistake" I hear you say. So what? Nobody will know it's a mistake accept yourself. I'll let you into a secret. I'm a bit of a perfectionist! But I've learned to accept the imperfections of watercolor painting. In fact, it's one of the things that make watercolors so interesting!

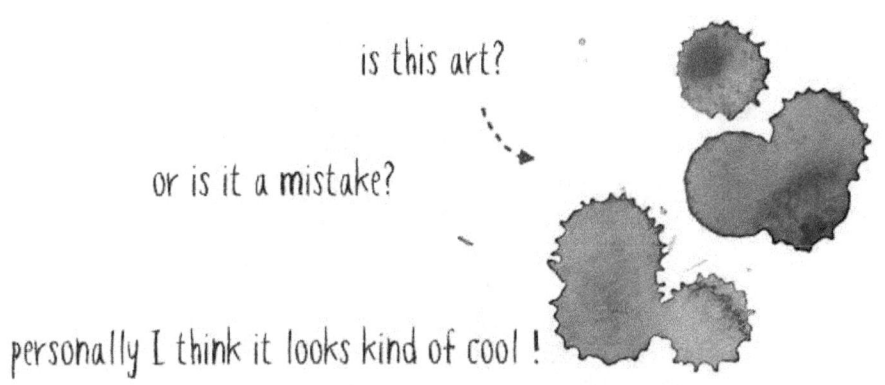

You don't feel creative

As a child you drew without concern. The thing is, you've always been creative... You've just forgotten this part of yourself.
Every new painting is a step towards improving your skills and finding your creative voice.
I find the best way to overcome doubt is to take action. Practicing watercolors, just a little every day, is a great way to dissipate doubt.
And remember this is supposed to be fun!

Lack of time

Luckily for you, watercolors are highly accessible. Watercolors are very portable, so you can take them just about anywhere. A sketchbook and a portable watercolor palette take up very little space, so you can enjoy painting whenever you take a break from everyday life. In a café, on your lunch break, in the park, on your kitchen table...
The opportunities are there if you look for them.

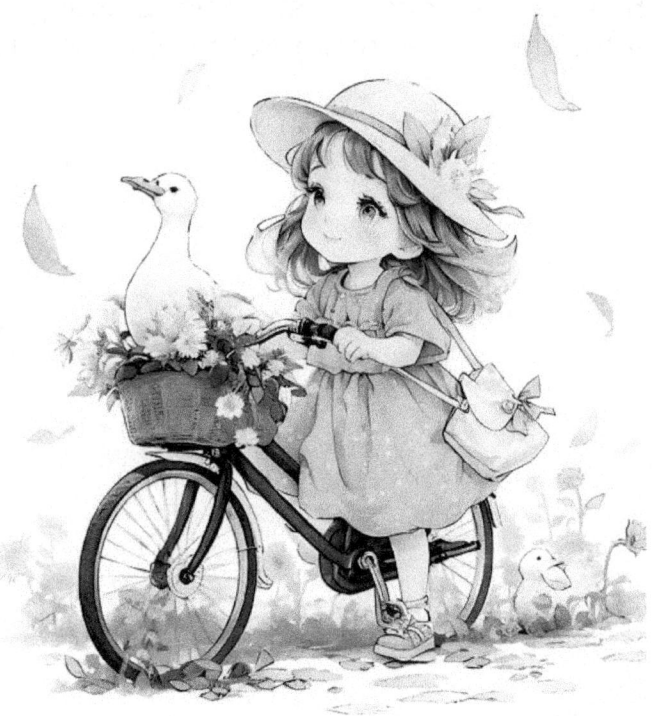

Understanding watercolor paint

Beginners often don't know how to use watercolor paints and what to expect from this extraordinary art medium. Maybe you've already painted using another type of paint like acrylic. Or this could be the first time you pick up a brush.
Watercolor paint is endlessly rewarding. But it has a very playful nature. Pigment and water often do what they like.

They blend together to produce gorgeous patterns of color. But watercolor is also transparent. And transparent paint leaves every brushstroke visible.

For these reasons watercolors have the reputation of being difficult to learn and control. I think that's a bit unfair. You might have an accident with your brush. But these happy accidents should be seen as an opportunity not a mistake. This way you'll get greater enjoyment from the painting process.

The fundamental thing to understand about watercolor is hidden in its name.

Water...
The wetness and the flow of water, and the transparent characteristics this creates, are what determine the outcome of your paintings. The rule to remember is this. **Water will always flow from wet to less wet.** An area of wet paint will seek equilibrium and flow towards the area of lesser wetness. The water carries pigments from one place to another. And water evaporates and dries quickly. So your window of opportunity for playing with the paint is sometimes short (that's why I try to use plenty of water in my mixes and keep colored washes wet while working).

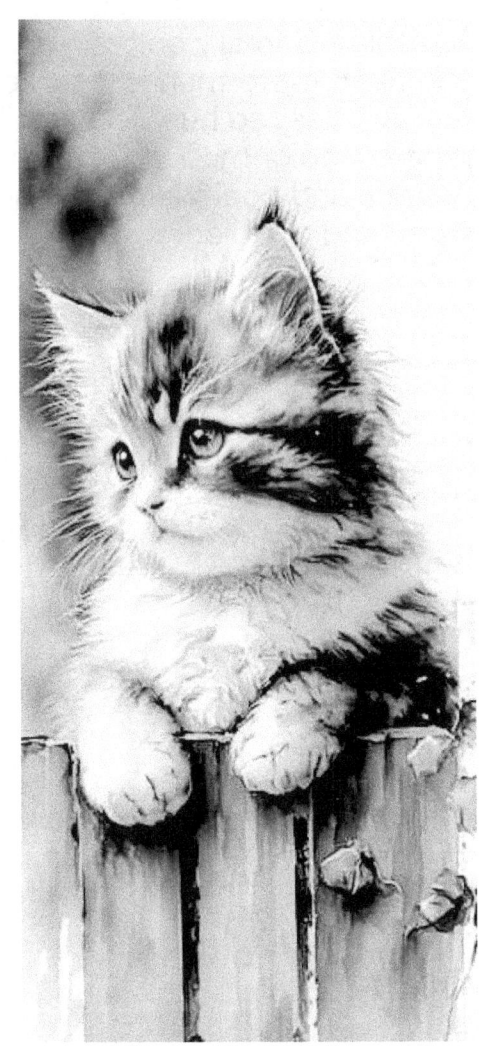

What you need to Start with Watercolors

You don't need much to start painting. The basics include a brush, watercolor paper, and a few paints. And you don't need a huge range of colors to get great results.

Basic color theory tells us that you can mix any color from just three primary colors: **yellow, red, and blue.** In reality you need more than just three primary colored paints to mix any desired hue. The smallest palette for the best range of color mixing consists of **six colors**.
A warm and cool **yellow**, a warm and cool **blue**, and a warm and cool red.

cool yellow   warm yellow   cool red

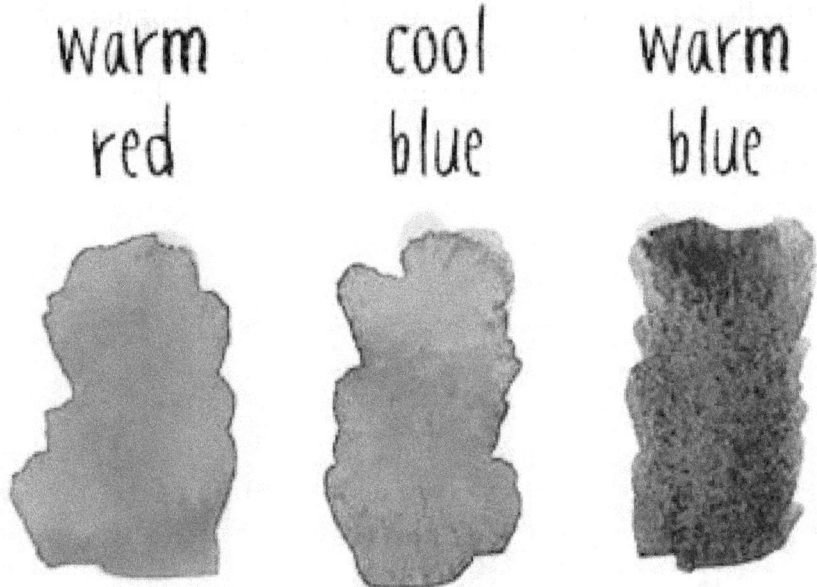

In general, you can define warm colors as those that tend towards red and cool colors are those that tend towards blue. Cool paints contain pigments that are more blue, and warm paints use pigments that tend toward red. Unfortunately "pure" primary pigment colors don't exist, so you need a combination of cool and warm primaries to balance each other, and to get a full range of color variations in your mixes.

Next you need a brush. Watercolor brushes are designed to work specifically well with water. They have a good pointed tip for accuracy, and they hold a lot of water (they have what is referred to as a good reservoir). The very best type of watercolor brushes are made of natural hair, because they have the best characteristics. But these can be expensive. The most affordable alternative is a mix of natural and synthetic bristles. The "Silver Brush" company make some good brushes of this kind.

Try to find a medium sized round brush to begin with. A size 8 round is a good option. Round brushes are the most versatile and allow a wide range of brushstrokes. And if your brush is too small you'll waste a lot of time picking up paint, and it will limit your brushwork.

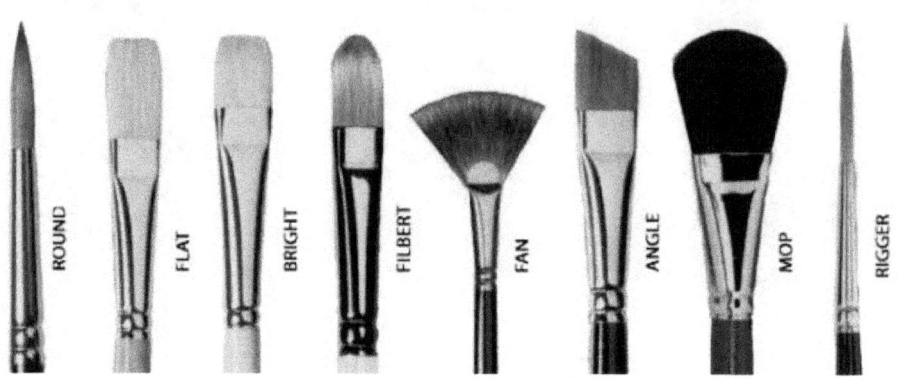

Watercolor paper is a necessity, because any other kind of paper won't handle the wet paint very well. High quality 100% cotton paper can be pricey. But you can get perfectly good student grade paper which is sufficient to begin with. Just make sure the paper is reasonably thick. A good minimum weight is 140 lb / 300 gsm.

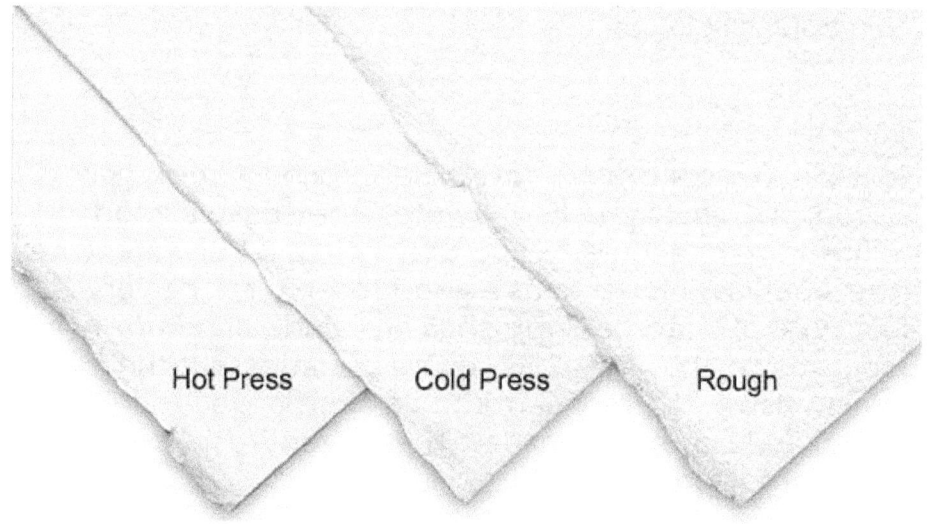

What to paint to get started?

This isn't a tutorial about every possible watercolor technique available. That would take a long time to explain. But the idea here is to get started with watercolor paints. Hopefully, you'll find the projects below are a good way to start exploring the nature of watercolors, and at the same time discover that it's possible to create appealing artwork with simple ideas.
You don't need to be a naturally talented artist to enjoy this art medium.

Watercolor Feathering Starter Tutorial

> This little painting uses a technique called feathering. It's a fun way to discover the way paints behave in relation to water. It combines wet paint on dry paper, and wet paint over wet paper, which are both typical techniques in watercolor painting.

Set yourself up with your supplies and two jars of water. This isn't essential, but it's a good idea to have two sources of water: one for rinsing your brush, and one with clean water for mixing. You'll also need a mixing palette for preparing your colors. Some watercolor box sets have built-in palettes. Otherwise you can just use a white plate

(white is best because otherwise you can't make out the colors properly).

Before you start painting you need to mix some paint. Choose any color you like. Begin by getting your brush nice and wet so that it soaks up plenty of liquid. Then load it with water and press it against you mixing palette to release a puddle of water. Make a nice big puddle.

f you're using tubes, squeeze out some paint onto the palette. Now stroke your moist brush across the paint and load it with pigment.

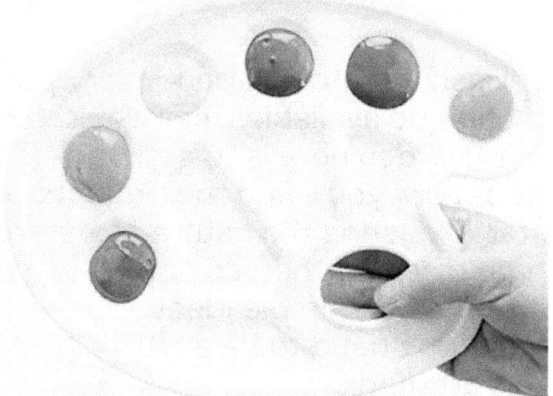

Gently mix the pigment into the puddle of water. Mix well to create a smooth blend. You can test the strength of your color on a spare sheet of paper. If it's too strong add more water. If it's too light, add more pigment (keep in mind that when watercolor paint dries it has a lighter toned appearance than when it's wet). Try to get a medium strength mixture, not too dark and not too light.
- Now clean your brush to remove all the colored paint. Begin the painting by loading your brush with clear water and paint 4 or 5 parallel lines onto the paper, leaving a gap between each line. You'll see why you're doing this in a minute. You don't want these lines to be soaking wet, but just damp (wait a minute if you think it's too moist).
- Once the paper has been wetted with linear brushstrokes, load your brush with colored paint. Now apply linear strokes at right angles to your damp lines. Repeatedly paint a pattern of lines, one under the other, leaving a space between each.
- As you paint the colored lines you'll see the pigments of your watercolors dispersing sideways into the wet paper lines, creating a feather-like texture.

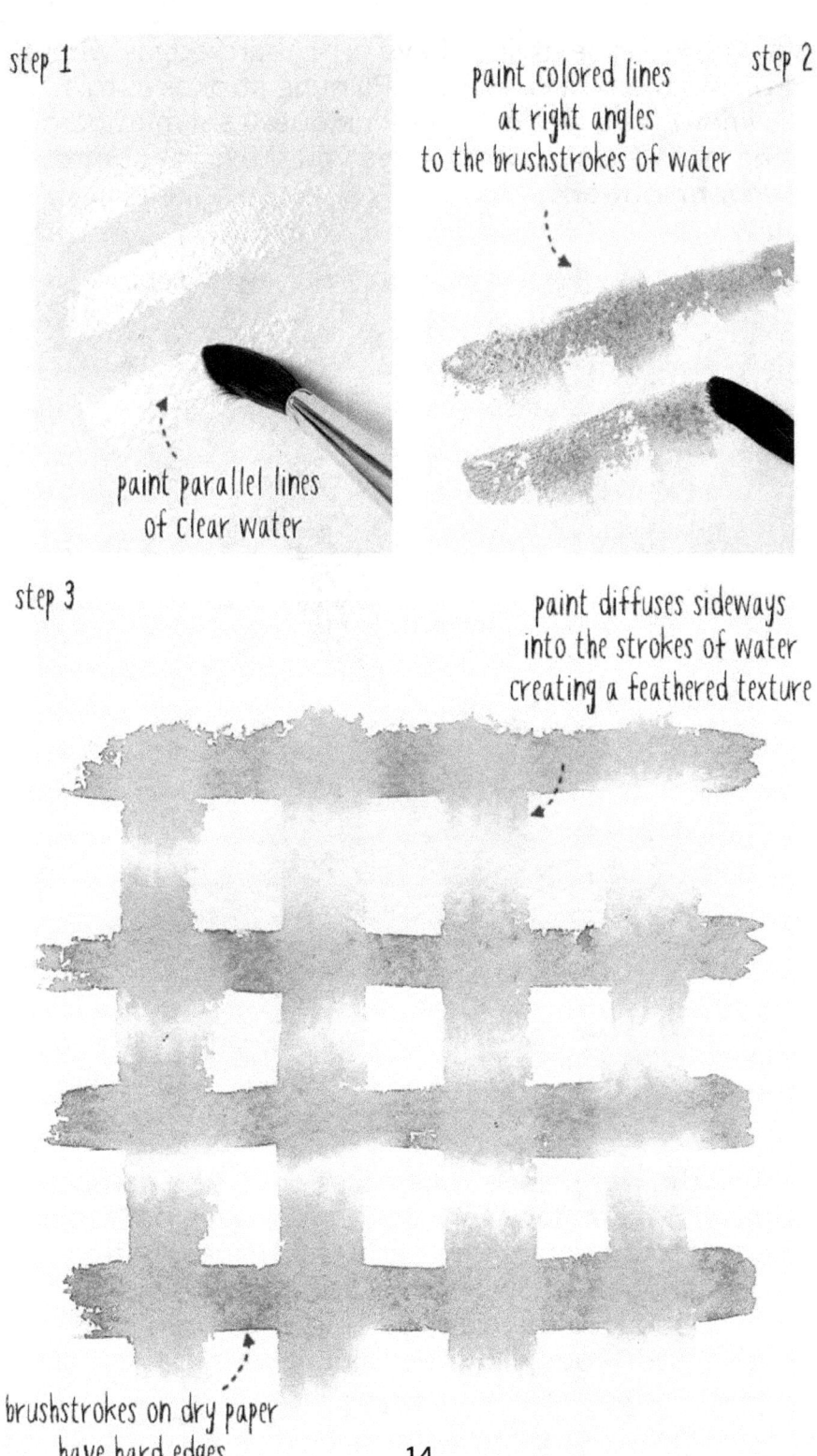

Notice how your paint lines have crisp, hard edges where you applied them to dry paper. Painting strokes in this way is known as a wet on dry technique. It's a method of painting in watercolor which gives you the most control over your brushwork.

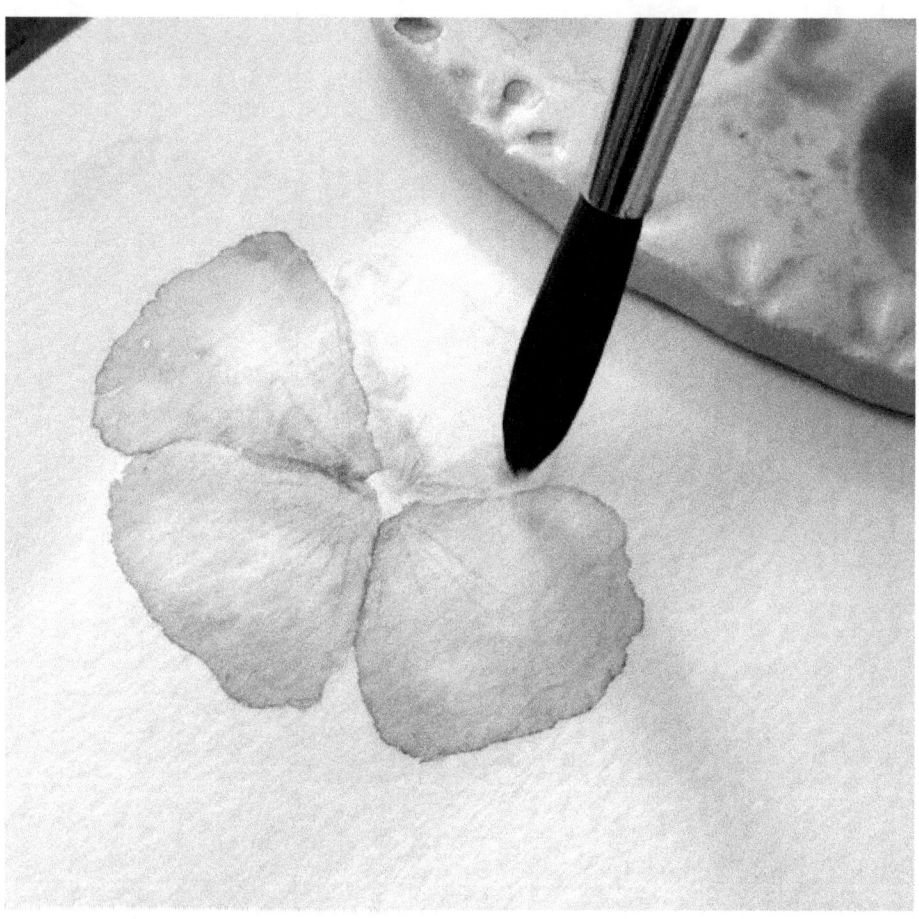

Each time the wet paint stroke passes over the damper lines, the wet paint flows into the damp paper, producing a diffused effect (If you remember from the description above, water always flows from a wet wash towards a less wet wash). Because the clear water lines are damp, but not soaking wet, your juicy wet paint flows into the moist lines.

Simple watercolor flowers with layered paint

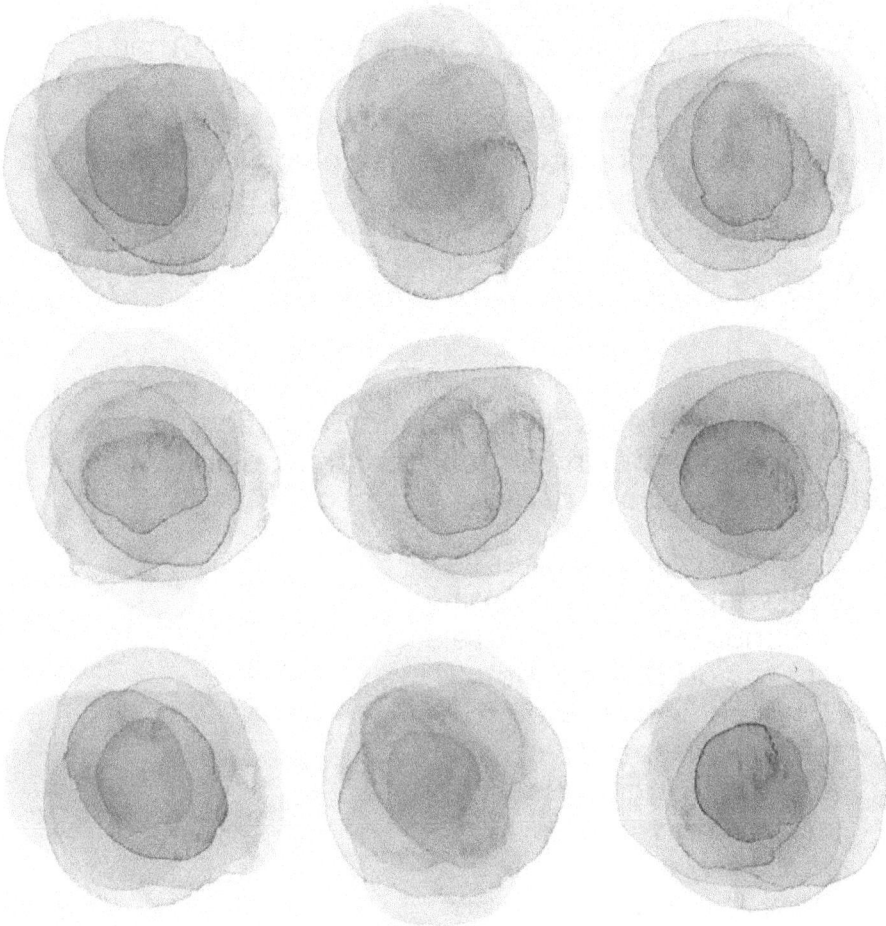

Make your colors quite diluted. Remember, watercolor paints are transparent, and you want to exploit this to your advantage.

For this next project I'm using a limited palette of three primary colors and to keep things simple there's no mixing. By limiting the number of colors in your paintings you stand a better chance of achieving harmonious results. Too many colors often look confusing and can conflict with each other. I selected a warm yellow, and a warm and cool red. Like this I'm also using colors which are close to each other on the color wheel (a color wheel is a kind of chart which artists use to help them with color mixing and color design). Using hues that are close to each other is known as an analogous color design.

You'll see the effects of this transparency in this easy exercise (Some beginners mix very thick paint which defeats the purpose of using watercolor).

- Begin by painting a series of oval shapes. I'm alternating the orientation of my ovals just to add some variety. Now you need to wait for the oval washes to dry. This is important, because if you start painting over a previously laid wash too soon, the underlying paint will lift and smudge the first shape.
- Now paint a new series of oval shapes over the top of the first. Use different colors, and again you can alternate the orientation of the ovals so that they overlap the edges of the first shapes.

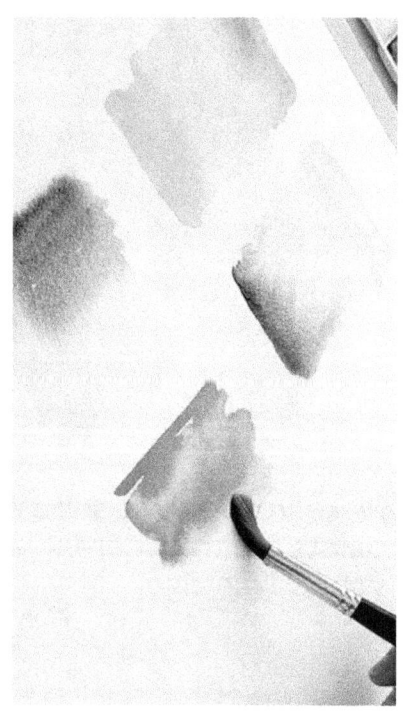

Notice how the underlying oval shape remains visible. Also with each new layer of paint you increase the intensity of the color, and the two colors combine to create a new blended color. This is most noticeable when you overlap yellow on red, resulting in an orange appearance.

The painting technique you are using is called glazing, which basically means layering washes of paint on top of each other after they have dried.

- Let the paint dry again, then paint some new ovals into the existing shapes. Make them slightly smaller, and change the colors and orientation each time.
- Repeat the process again and again until you're happy with the result You'll end up with a pattern of abstract watercolor "flowers".

Cool... Huh?

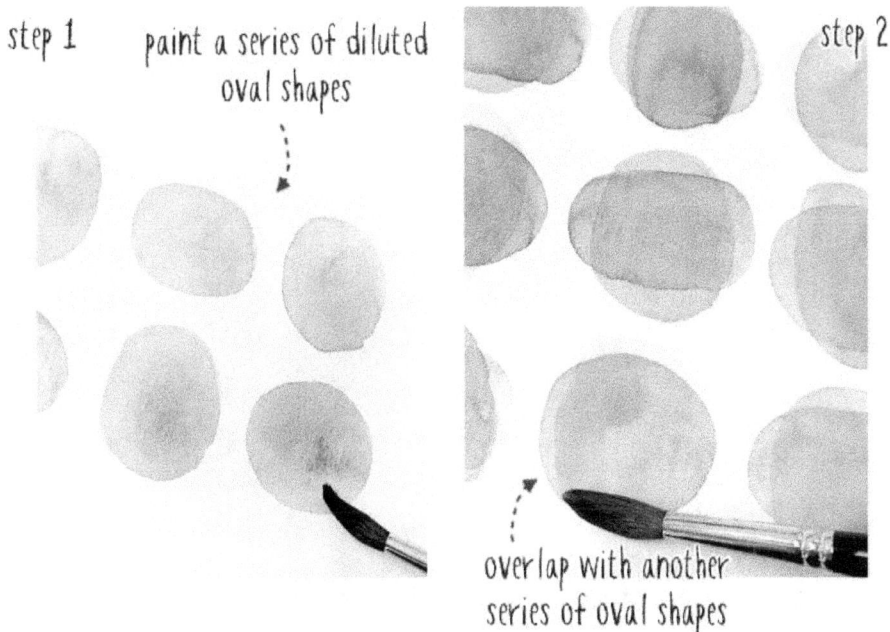

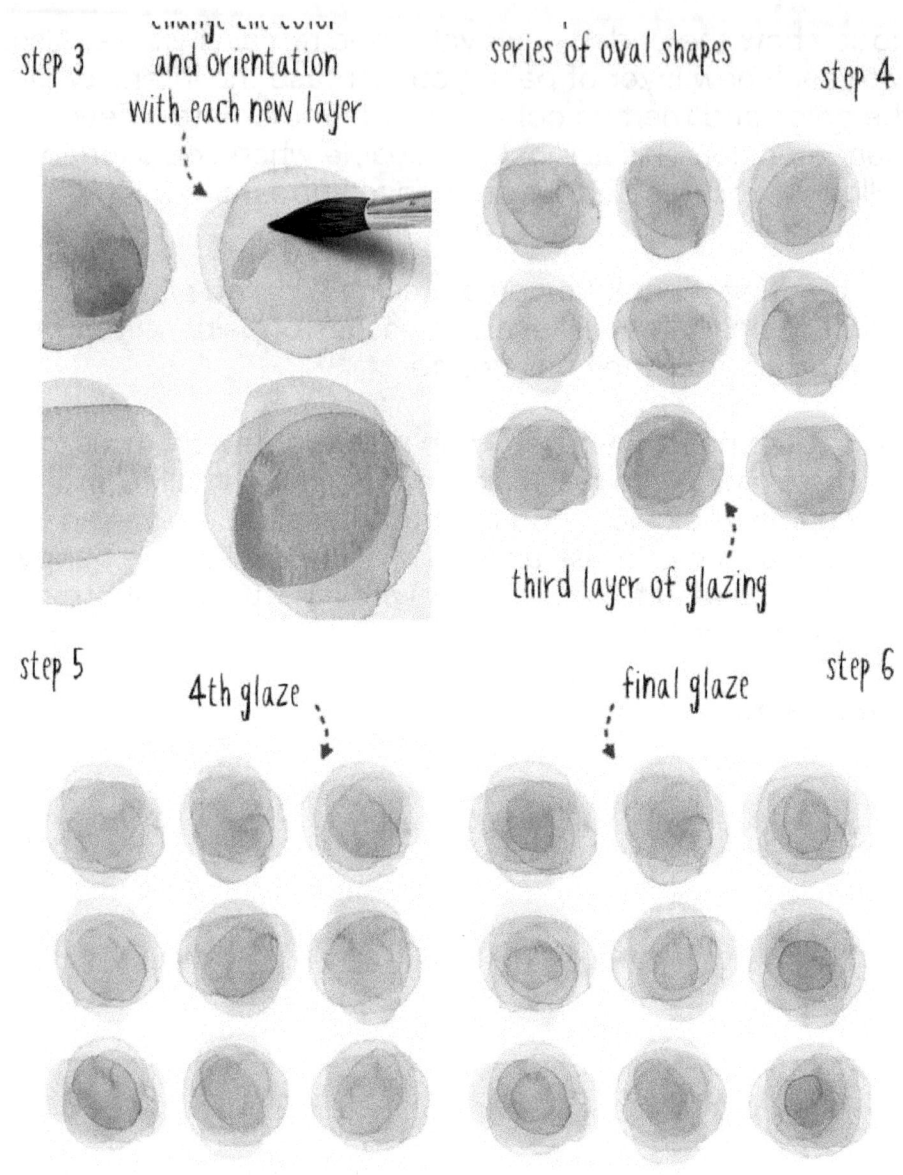

Beginners color mixing tutorial with warm & cool primary paints

In this simple painting you're going to discover why you need six primary colored paints to achieve a good range of color mixing.

Begin by drawing two squares on your paper. In the first square you're going to paint washes of **cool colors**, and in the second you will paint washes of **warm colors**. Prepare a good wet mixture of all six primary colors in your palette. The idea here is to work quickly, because you want to apply all three primary colors into each square before the first washes start to dry. This is a technique called **wet on wet**, and as you will see, it produces beautiful diffused blends of color.

- Start by wetting the square with clear water. You want the colors to blend together on the paper, and this is easier if the surface remains wet while you're working. This is a painting technique known as wet on wet.
- In the first square you will be combining cool yellow, cool blue, and cool red. It's a good idea to start with your lightest toned colors, which in general is yellow (this is because yellow gets easily contaminated with darker colors from your brush or on your palette). Fill in one corner of the square.
- Next add some cool blue on the other side of the square. Let the paints diffuse and mix together on the paper.
- Finally add some cool red to complete the square. You can encourage the paints to blend together by tilting the paper slightly, or by dabbing color into the wet wash to create mixes on the surface.
- Go through the same process with the other square, only this time you will use only Warm yellow, warm blue, and warm red.

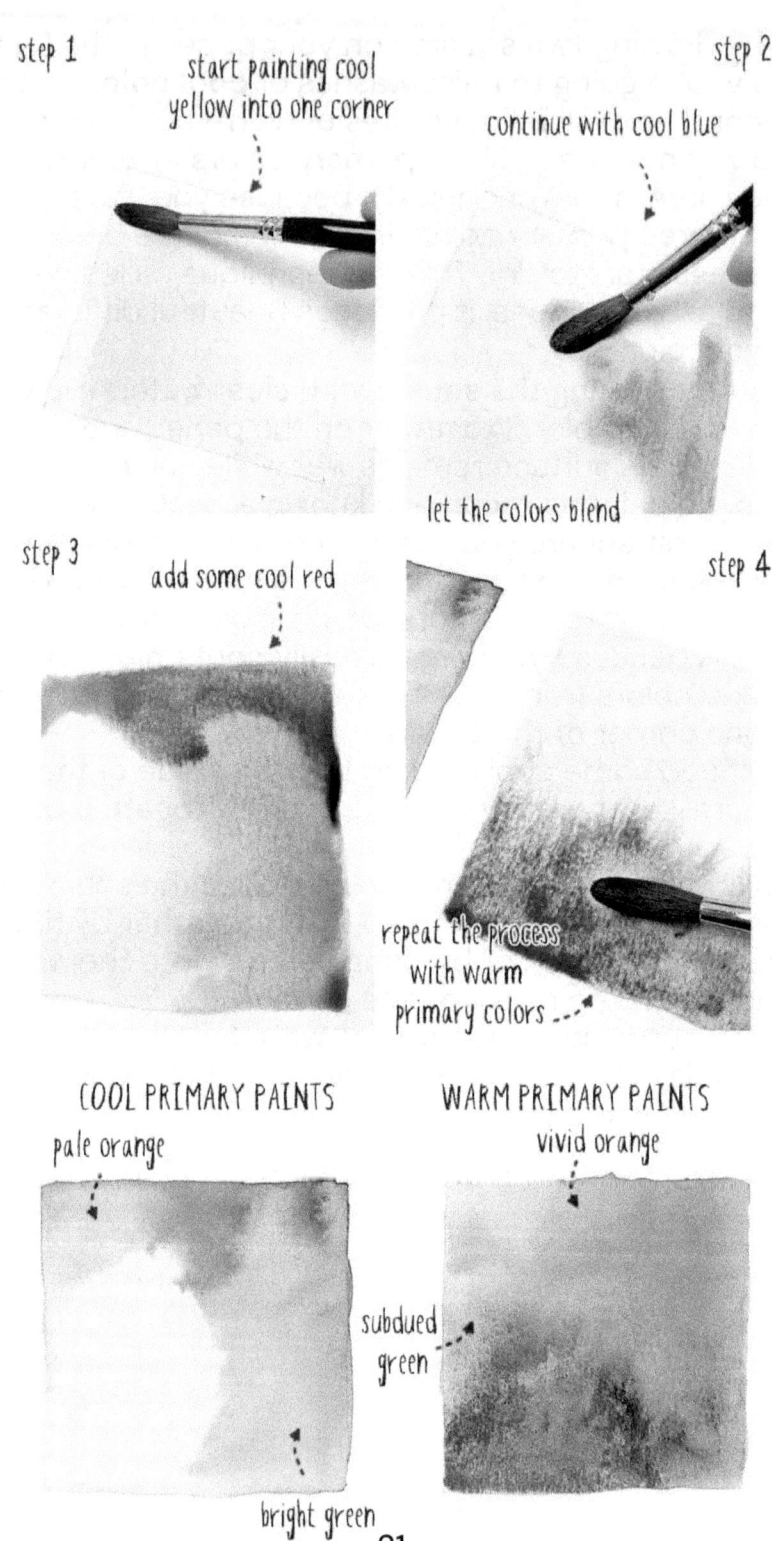

Notice the difference between the two squares. Even though we used primary colors for each, the color appearance is completely different. For example, cool yellow and cool blue blend to make a nice bright green. On the other hand, warm yellow and warm blue produce a more subdued olive green mixture. The resulting purples and oranges are also very different.

Color mixing is an important skill in watercolor painting, but as you can see, it's possible to produce a huge range of fabulous colors even with a limited paint palette. Just imagine all the color variations you can create!
I hope this gives you some insight into the wonderful world of watercolors. But keep in mind, the secret to watercolor painting is practice!
The more you paint, the more competent you become, and the faster you grow as an artist.
Go grab those brushes!

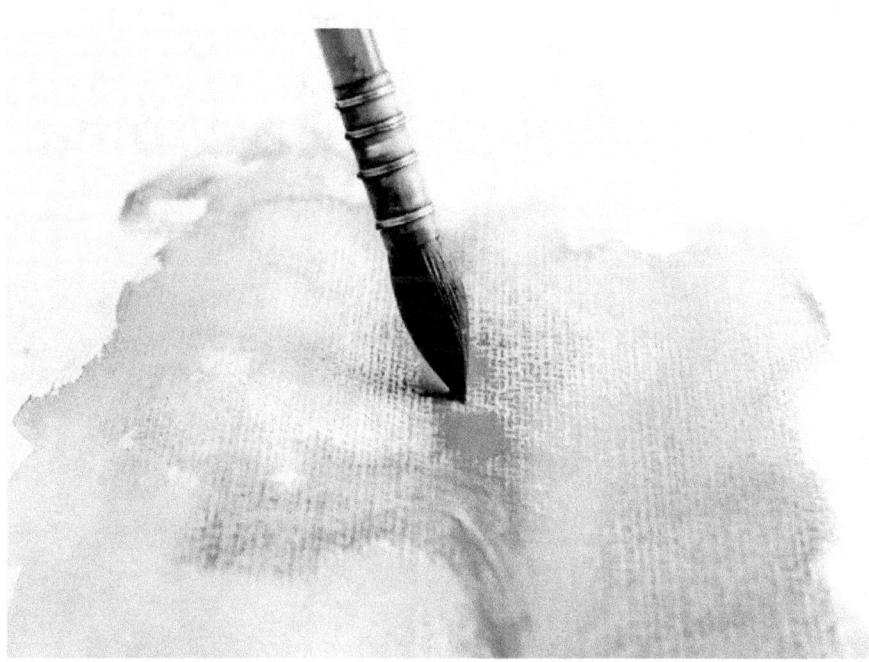

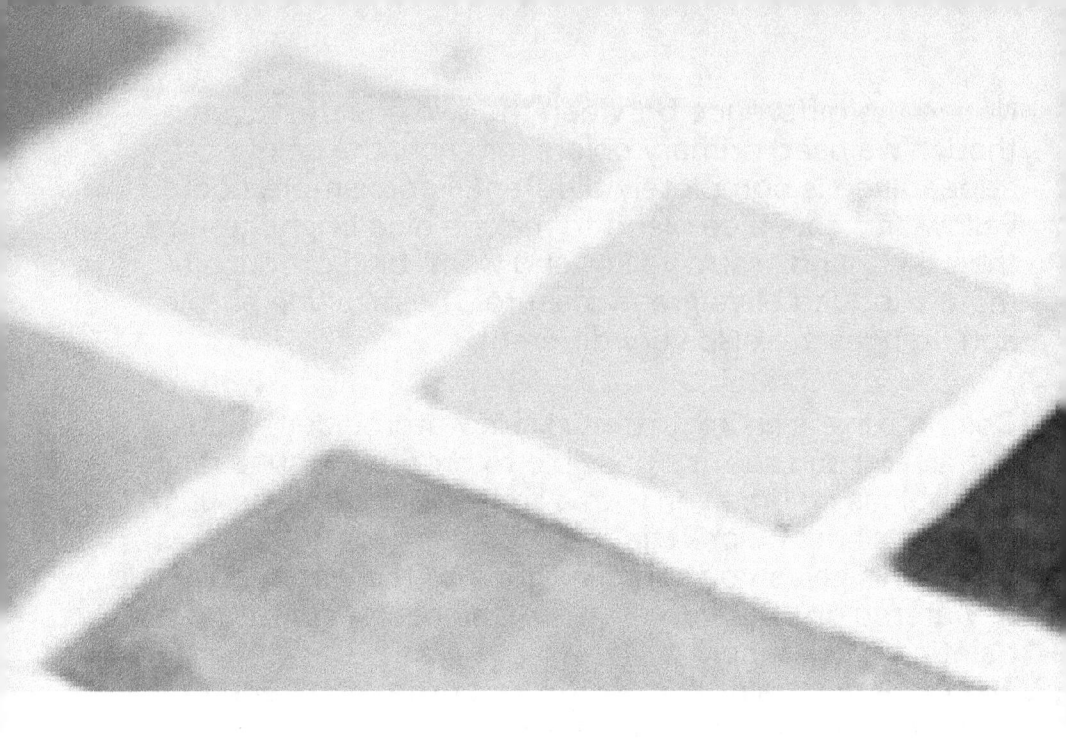

Guide to recommended watercolor palette colors

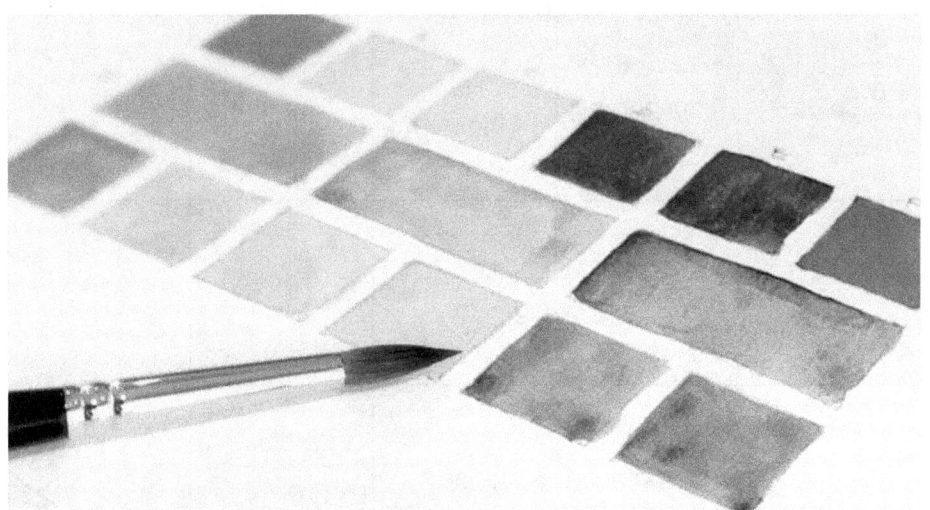

I hear it all the time!

What color paints do you recommend?

This is something that I agonized over when I first started painting with watercolors!

The choice of paint colors is staggering, especially when you consider watercolor brands like Daniel Smith (they have a huge collection of over 250 paints!)

And good quality watercolors are expensive! I didn't want to make a mistake and buy colors that I wouldn't use!

I even made a spreadsheet comparing the recommendations of various well known artists... Argh!

In the end I created a list of recommended watercolor palette colors, and this is what it looked like:

> Notes: GS = green shade BS = blue shade.
> Pigment numbers begin with "P" for pigment, then another letter to denote each color.
> For example, PY means pigment = yellow. PO means pigment = orange. PR means pigment = red, etc.

Color	Transparency	No. of Pigments	Pigment	
Lemon Yellow	Transparent	Single pigment	PY175	
New Gamboge	Transparent	2 pigments	PY97 & PY110	
Transparent Pyrrol Orange	Transparent	Single pigment	PO71	
Pyrrol Scarlet	Semi-transparent	Single pigment	PR255	
Quinacridone Rose	Transparent	Single pigment	PV19	
Pyrrol Crimson	Semi-transparent	Single pigment	PR264	
Quinacridone Violet	Transparent	Single pigment	PV19	

Name	Transparency	Pigment Count	Pigment
French Ultramarine	Transparent	Single pigment	PB29
Phthalo Blue (GS)	Transparent	Single pigment	PB15:3
Prussian Blue	Transparent	Single pigment	PB27
Phthalo Green (BS)	Transparent	Single pigment	PG7
Yellow Ochre	Transparent	Single pigment	PY43
Raw Sienna	Semi-transparent	Single pigment	PBr7
Quinacridone Burnt Orange	Transparent	Single pigment	PO48
Burnt Sienna	Semi-transparent	Single pigment	PBr7
Burnt Umber	Semi-transparent	Single pigment	PBr7

There's a total of 16 colors above. Now... you don't have to get as many colors to get started. And I'll tell you how you can get by with less colors if you want. But I came up with this list as a result of hours of research.
Let me explain...

How to choose palette colors

The perfect color palette doesn't exist.
Unfortunately, there isn't some stupefying list of flawless watercolor paints, (wouldn't that be great...)
In the end it comes down to personal styles and preferences, and a good understanding of your watercolor paints.
Different watercolorists will have different recommendations. But when you begin to compare other artists preferences, you start to see some similarities and certain colors that crop up often.
Nevertheless, there are a few basic rules that most watercolor artists stick to for choosing a basic palette of colors.

Must have watercolors – warm and cool primary colors

Primary colors are a must have because they cannot be mixed from other colors. You probably already know that you can mix any color you need from just the primary colors, red, yellow and blue.
At least that's the theory.
In reality the color you obtain from the paint is dependant on the pigment it contains. And when you consider primary color paints more closely they can have a warm or cool hue depending on the pigment used.
As a result, when you mix three cool primary colors you get quite a different result compared to when you mix three warm primary colors. Below are a few examples...

Warm primary color chart

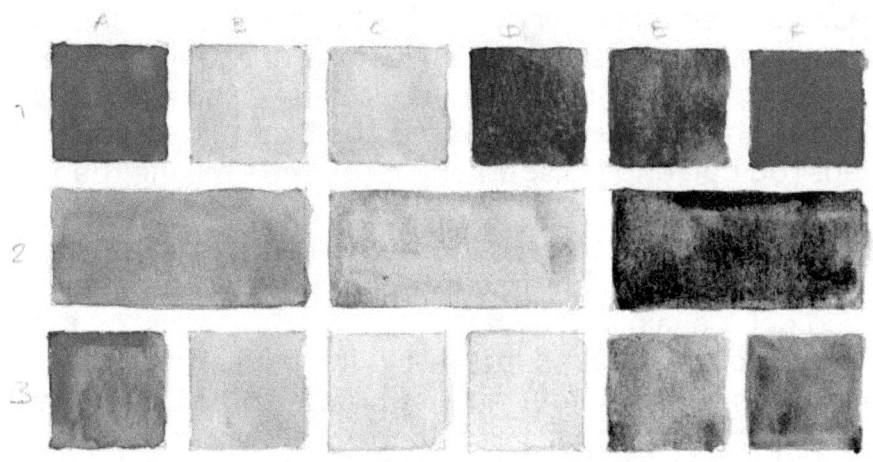

Cool primary color chart

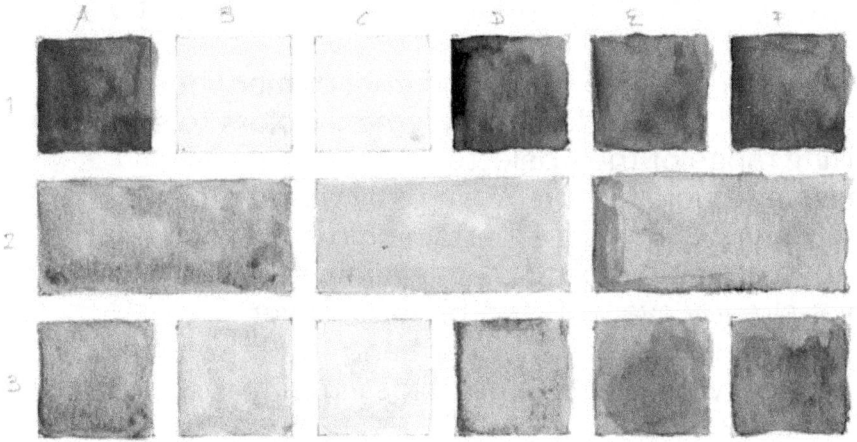

The colors used in these charts are as follows:
- *lemon yellow (cool) / new gamboge (warm)*
- *Quinacridone Rose (cool) / Pyrrol Scarlet (warm)*
- *Phthalo Blue (GS) (cool) / french ultramarine (warm)*

Having a mixture of both warm and cool primary colors in your palette is a terrific start to your palette, and with these you can mix a very useful set of colors.

If you're brave enough you can just make do with some primary colors. But the reality is, you need to really know your paints extremely well to mix the exact color you need. You can end up spending more time mixing than painting!

And you also need to be quite skilled in order to get the proportions right each time when you need the same mixed color again and again.

Mixing colors is an almost an art in itself and it is a very good investment of your time to create some color charts with your paints so you get to know what you can do with them.

Complimentary colors

You can create an abundance of colors with just a small number of paints.

In addition to some warm and cool primary colors most artists add a few additional pigment colors to extend the mixing range of their palette.

These additional colors are mostly for comfort and convenience. There are certain colors that so common that you end up mixing them again and again. Having a color already available is a big time saver.

Phthalo Green is a very vibrant and highly saturating color to have in your palette and helps simplify the mixing of other colors.

For example, Phthalo Green mixed with Pyrrol Crimson is an easy way to make an attractive black. Phthalo Green mixed with Yellow Ochre will result in an excellent Sap Green.

Quinacridone pigment paints are transparent and very vibrant. There are many varieties of colors using this pigment, but Quinacridone Violet is fantastic for making glowing purples.

Earth colors such as Raw Sienna and Burnt Sienna are also remarkably useful, and also help produce interesting greys. Browns are wonderful for landscapes, figures and skin tones. It is incredibly useful to have a ready to go dark brown in your palette such as Burnt Umber.
Quinacridone Burnt Orange is a very versatile neutral warm tone.

Which type of watercolor paints are best?

As you add colors to your palette you should first consider the quality of the paint you are choosing. Most artists will agree that the three key factors to choosing good quality paint are transparency, the number of pigments used to make a particular color, and its lightfastness.

Transparent watercolor paints

When you start looking closely at the labels on watercolor paint you'll find that not all watercolor paint has the same transparency value. In general, paint can be transparent, semi-transparent or opaque.
This transparency affects the appearance of your paintings.
You may notice that certain watercolors have a milky or chalky appearance when dried. This happens in particular when you use opaque paints.
Why is this important?
With watercolor painting, the brightness of the colors is mostly the result of light reflecting off the white paper support. In addition, most watercolorists build up successive layers or glazes of paint to achieve the final result.
When you apply 2 or 3 glazes of opaque paint, this covers the surface of the paper and less light is reflected from the white paper surface.
The outcome is colors that are less vivid.
You can test the transparent properties of your paint by...

Single pigment watercolor paints

You can combine single pigments to mix the rest of your colors and achieve much more satisfying results. When you mix too many pigments together the resulting color becomes murky and dull. This is why many experienced artists avoid paints that are pre-mixed with 2 or more pigments. **The fundamental rule** in watercolor mixing is **don't mix too many paints.**

Lightfastness

You can think of non-lightfast paints as temporary. Certain pigments when exposed to light for a certain duration will fade over time. The same is true for some other environmental factors such as pollution and humidity.
If you want your masterpieces to last as long as possible then you must choose lightfast paint. Check the labels and stick to pigments that have an "excellent" or "good" rating
Combining all of these quality characteristics together at the same time can be tricky. So creating a palette where every color is single pigment, transparent, with excellent lightfastness is near impossible!
So try to stick to these quality measures as closely as possible, but don't be afraid to make some compromises, as I did in with the recommended palette above.

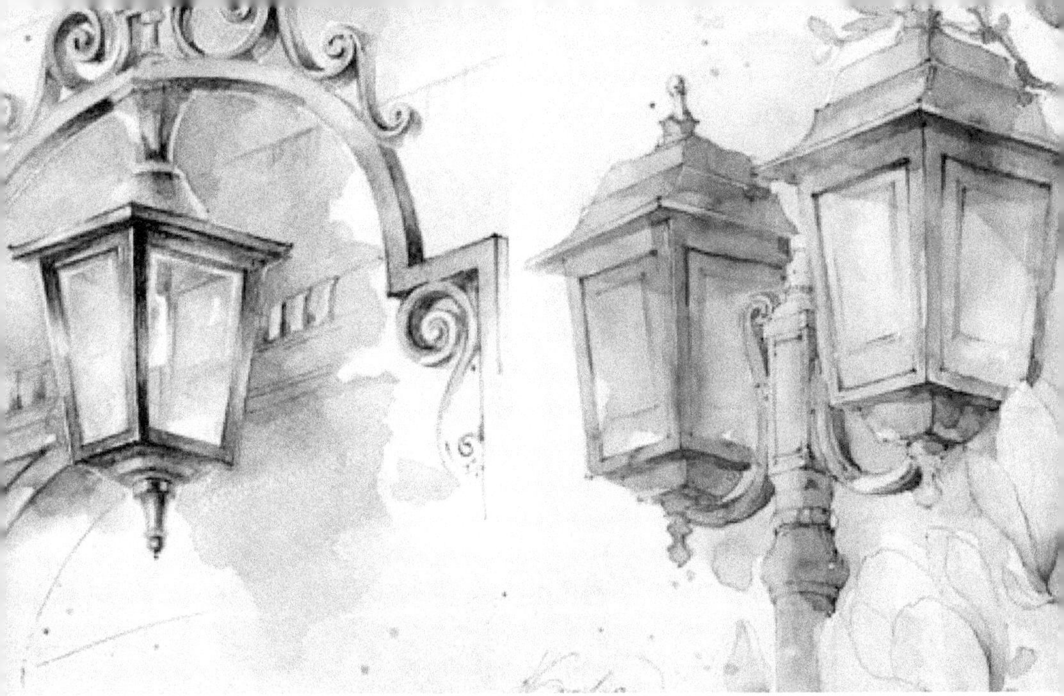

Beginners Step by Step Tutorial

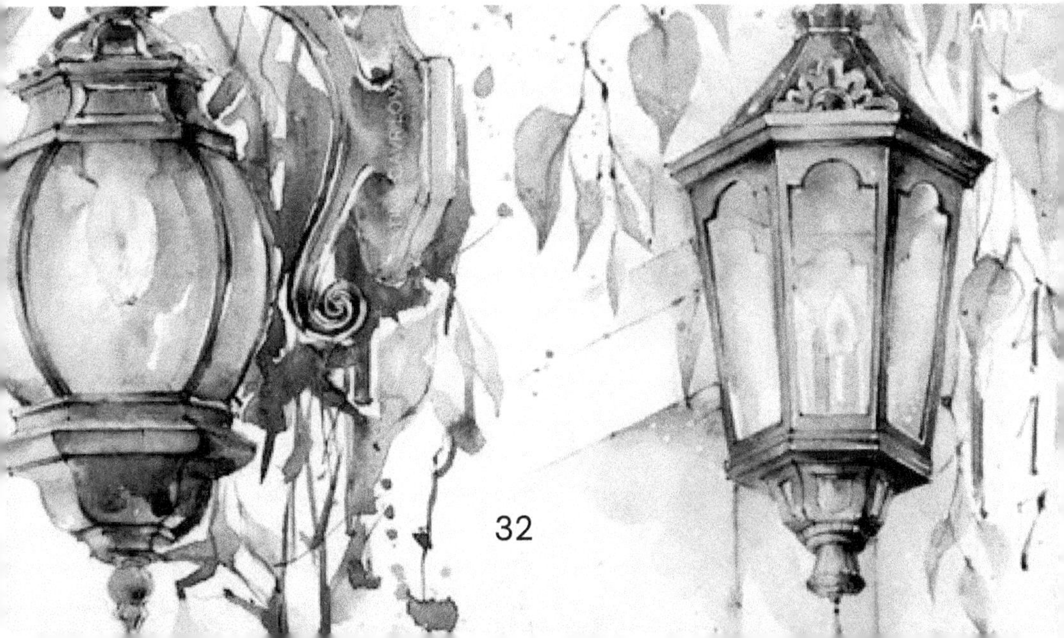

Watercolor Still Life

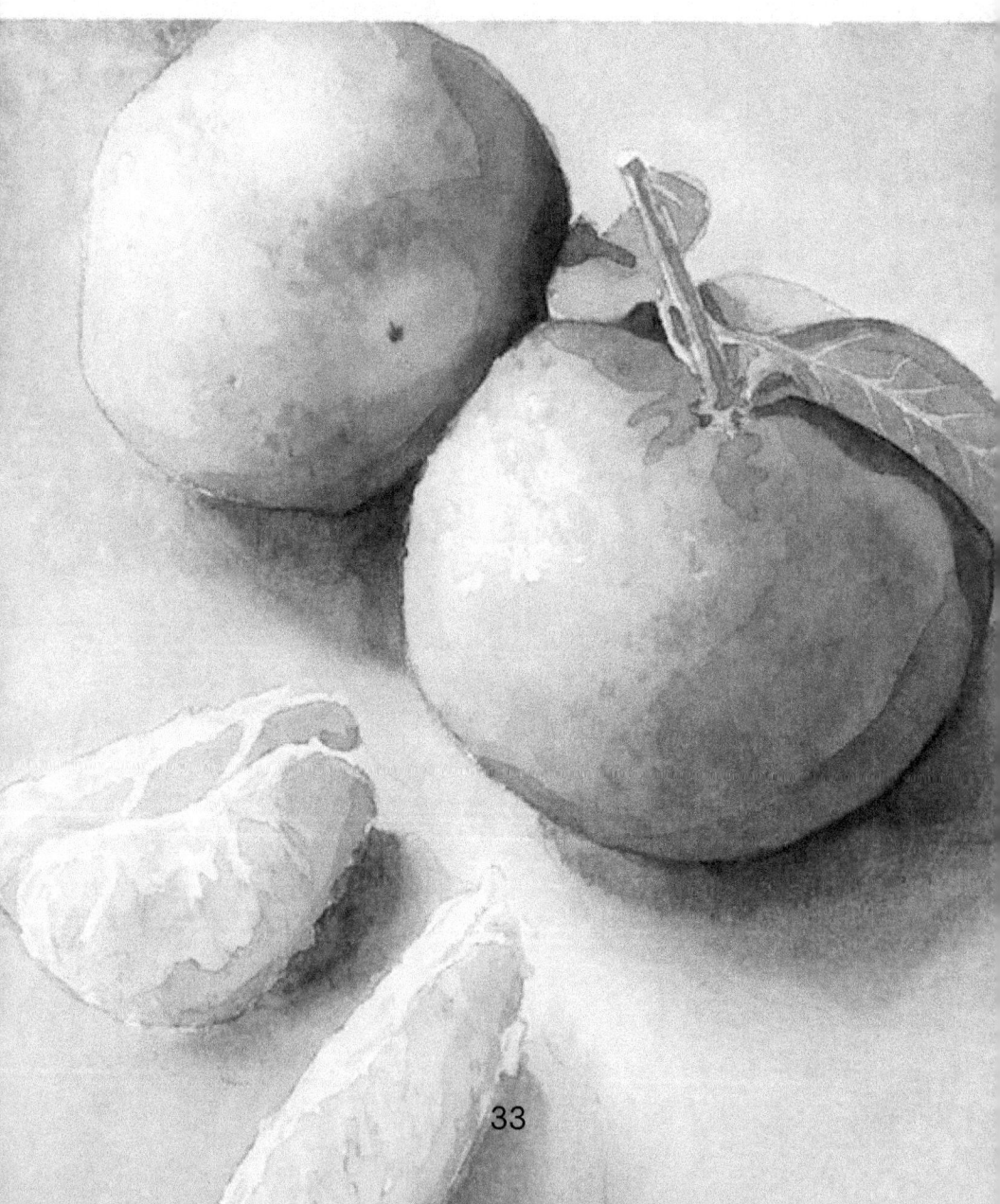

Watercolor Still Life

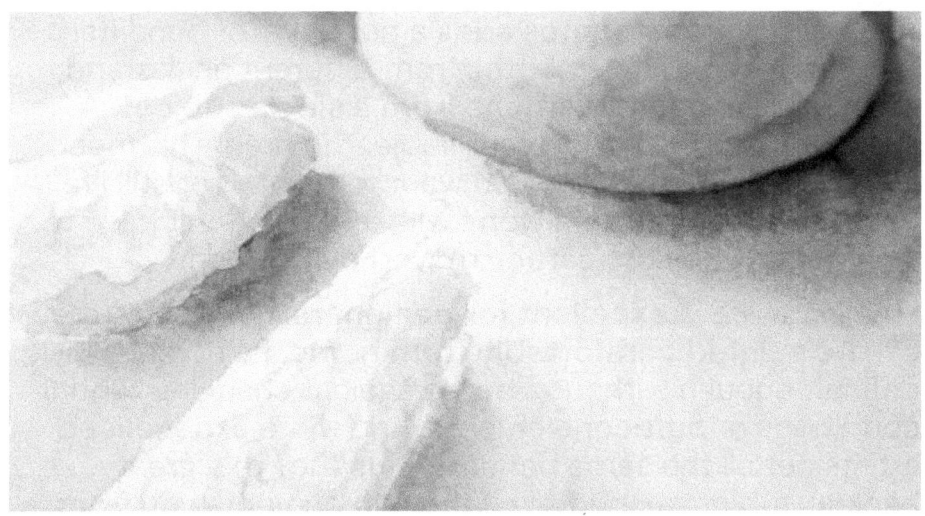

Did you ever wonder where the tradition of giving oranges at Christmas comes from?
Well... There are a few different versions, but one of the stories I seem to remember talks about how an orange represents the Christmas season of giving and sharing. This is because oranges can be split into segments and shared with others!
So, while I can't actually share a real orange with everybody, I can at least share this watercolor painting of an orange. *(actually this is a clementine, but shhh... just keep that to yourself, will you?)*

Watercolor Still Life

The advantages of still life in watercolor are considerable. However, what most artists love about still-life paintings is the amount of control they have.

Your subject can be arranged, lit, and set up in any way you like. You can move things around, change backgrounds, and find precisely the angle you want for a composition.

You can work directly from life or take a photo.

And painting from photos adds a new level of benefits! You can take multiple photos from different angles and get **numerous compositions from a single subject.** A snapshot also suspends your subject in time! This means you can take all the time you want to paint your still life because fruit or flowers won't wilt, and you don't have to worry about objects getting moved by accident.

I think still life is **excellent for beginners.** For a start, they can be painted **comfortably from home.** Painting is difficult enough without a battle against changing lighting conditions or outdoor elements. And more experienced artists get all the same benefits, plus they're a great backup subject, especially if the rain prevents you from getting out to paint.

Another non-negligible advantage is that you **don't have to render your subjects accurately** to get good results. If the proportions of your apples or that bottle aren't quite right, nobody's going to notice!

Convinced yet?

Here's a summary of the advantages of still life painting:
- High level of control over the subject
- Paint any time
- From photo or real life
- There's no hurry
- Paint from the comfort of home.
- Suitable for beginners and seasoned painters alike
- It doesn't have to be accurate

Watercolor Still Life Ideas

So what should you paint?
Finding inspiration can be tricky at the best of times. So begin by looking around you!
Do you have any old heirlooms or things you've collected over time? Are there any objects that hold a particular meaning for you?
For example, I know a lot of artists who begin their sketchbooks by painting their artist supplies.

Here are a few ideas on how to find still life inspiration:

- Look in the kitchen. This is an excellent source of interesting objects which anyone can relate to. Utensils, bowls, and cutlery, all make great subjects.
- Raid a junk shop or a thrift store. Aged and stressed objects generally have interesting forms and nice textures.
- Find some old tools. Ancient hammers and used brushes have a lot of history and character.
- Keep an eye out for attractive packaging or interesting-looking jars at the grocery store. Candies and cakes are great as well.
- Pick things up while you're outdoors, like leaves, twigs, bark, or rocks. Natural forms and textures make good still-life objects.
- Flowers and plants are classic subjects to paint.

Over time you can build up a collection of objects for still life paintings. This could provide you with endless compositions and painting ideas.

> Tips: Don't use too many objects when you set up your still life. Still-life paintings can quickly get confusing. Also, try to select things that relate to each other somehow. Then, your artwork will tell a more straightforward story.

Watercolor Still Life Painting Step by Step

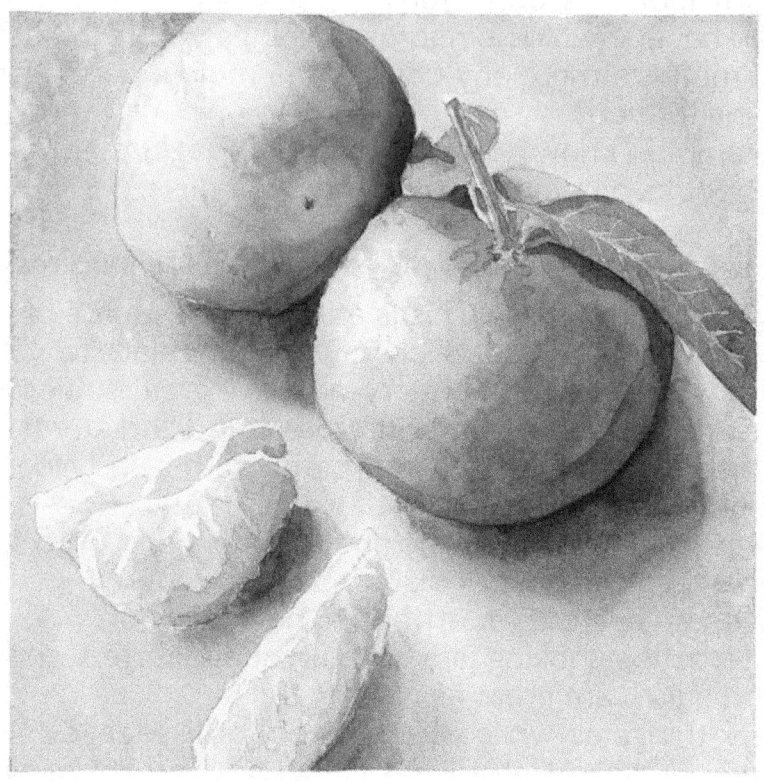

I'm going to take you through the step-by-step process I used to paint this watercolor still life from beginning to end.

If you want to follow along with this project, you can download the sketch template and my reference photo below.

The colors and supplies used in this exercise were as follows:
- Hansa Yellow Deep – Pigment number: PY65
- Phthalo Green BS – Pigment number: PG7
- French ultramarine – Pigment number: PB29

- Pyrrol scarlet – Pigment number: PR255
- Burnt Sienna – Pigment number: PBr7
- Arches Watercolor Pad 140 lb Cold Press (100% cotton Artist grade paper)
- Pebeo Masking Liquid
- Da Vinci Mop brush size 4 series 418
- Kolinsky Sable series 22 size 8 (short handle)

How to paint a watercolor still life

Begin by tracing the outline onto a sheet of watercolor paper. I'm using arches cold-press 140 lb / 300 gsm paper.

Next, fix the sheet onto a board using masking tape around all the edges. The masking tape defines the framing and cropping of the painting, so if you want the same composition, be careful to line up the masking tape the way I have in the sketch template.

The first thing I did was identify the brightest parts of the oranges and the orange segments and apply masking fluid to reserve the white paper. I'm using a bamboo dip pen for this.

Leave the masking fluid to dry completely then dampen the background with clear water, being careful to paint around the shapes of the oranges. I'm doing this so I can apply a wet-on-wet wash for the gray background color.

I chose to mix a cool gray color using burnt sienna and french ultramarine. I wanted the background to have a slightly blue tinge to set up a complementary color scheme with the oranges (Orange and blue create a color harmony which is said to be "complementary").

While this wash is still wet you can charge in some stronger paint into the areas of cast shadow. And to add some texture to the background, I used a spray bottle to splatter a few drops of clean water onto the damp wash.

Let the background drybefore painting the oranges, first with a diluted mix of warm yellow, then go back into the wash with a stronger mixture. The aim here is to begin establishing the tonal range, with light values around the highlights and stronger values toward the shaded side.

While the orange is still damp, continue to build up the value of the shaded side of the orange, with darker shades of orange paint. Use the reference photo as a guide to try and discern the bigger shapes of darker values.

Add some orange paint below the orange to represent the reflected light bouncing off the orange onto the surface underneath. Then leave this paint to dry before moving on to the next stage.

step 1

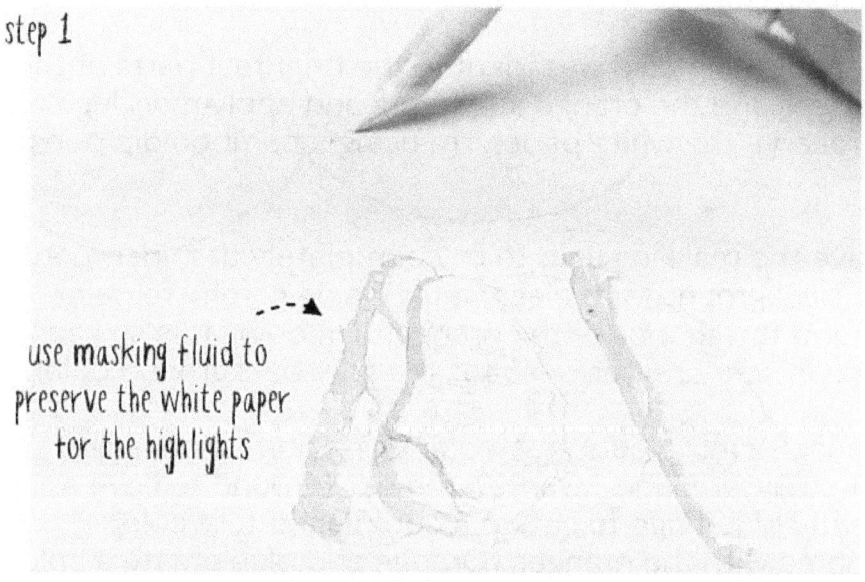

use masking fluid to preserve the white paper for the highlights

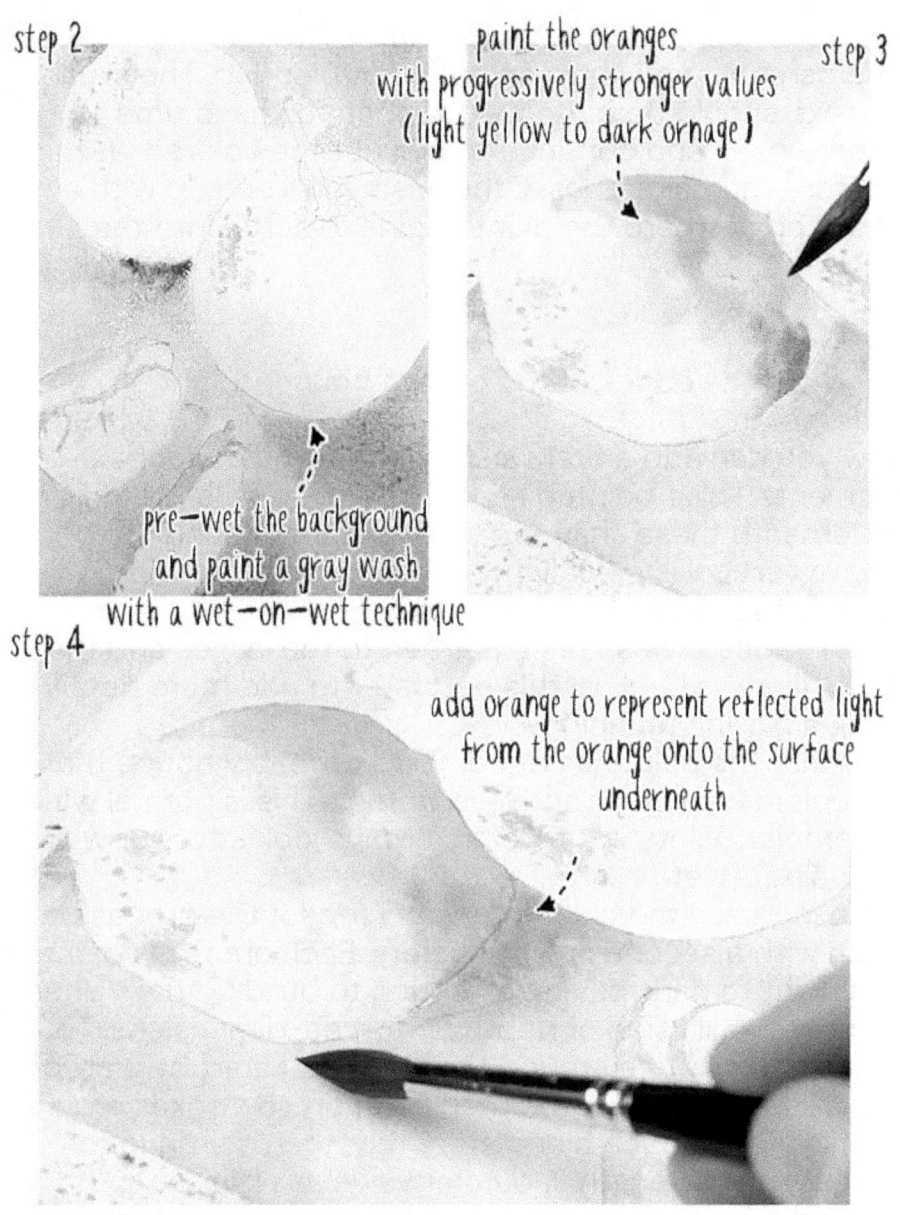

Apply the same approach to the second orange, being careful to paint around the leaf and stalk, and building up the tonal values to represent the spherical form. Begin with diluted yellow, then a stronger yellow mix, then orange, then darker orange, using a wet-on-wet technique so that the colors fuse together.

> Be careful if you leave an edge not blended. The brush stroke should be quite wet, so that you have time to come back and continue to pull out the colored wash before the paint dries. Otherwise you'll end up with a hard edge where the paint begins to settle into the paper.

Blend out the edges of the orange bounced light underneath.
Now you can add a first wash of color to the orange segments. I also painted a glow of orange color underneath these shapes. I used a lifting technique to create vertical lines of lighter color to simulate the textured veins on the segments.
Next I added a wash of light green to the leaves and the stalk. I'll come back to this part later to add more detail using a glazing technique.
Now that the paint has dried, you'll probably notice that the colors are lighter and less vibrant. This is normal with watercolor paints – the colors always look stronger while the paint is wet.
So to increase the color intensity I repeat the process again with a second layer of colors. Each orange is painted from light to dark, paying attention to build up the values to create an illusion of depth and three-dimensions. To avoid a harsh edge around the highlight I start by wetting the area with clear water, then I add brush strokes around the highlights which blend smoothly, then continue to increase the strength and color value as I progress.
I added a new glaze of color to the orange segments, but this time painting details to represent the textured pattern on their surface.
Leave this layer of paint to dry completely then you can remove the masking fluid using a kneaded eraser or a rubber cement pick-up tool.
In an attempt to improve the mottled texture of the

orange peel, I used a natural sponge dipped into paint, and dabbed onto the surface. You only need to do this in a few places to subtly improve the textured effect.

The final stage of this painting is to add some stronger shadows. Begin by adding some shadow details around the stalk, then add some stronger form shadows to the oranges themselves.

If you like you can use a dry sponge to mop up some of the paint and create a mottled edge to the shadow shape. I added a few darker details to the bottom of the segments near the shadow.

Then I started adding stronger cast shadows underneath the oranges themselves. I used french ultramarine neutralized with a small amount of burnt sienna. I wanted the shadows to have a blue hue to continue the complementary color scheme.

Don't forget to add some cast shadows on the oranges themselves, created by the stalk and leaves, and also in the extreme corners where the two oranges meet.

Then add the cast shadows under the segments as well.

step 5

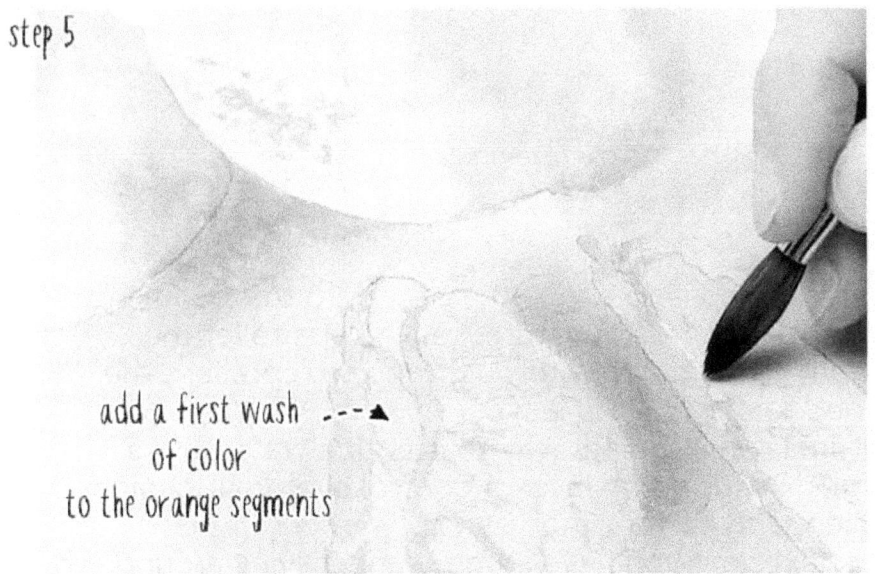

add a first wash of color to the orange segments

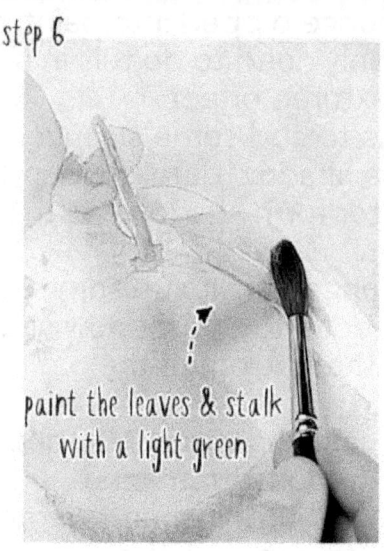
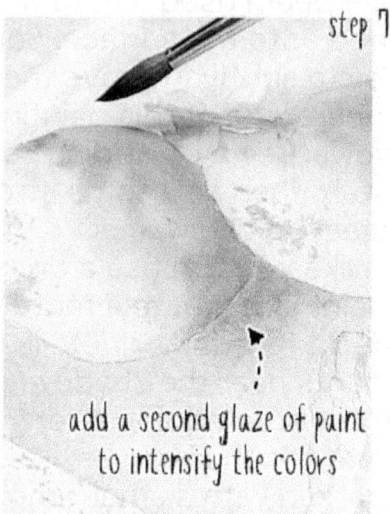
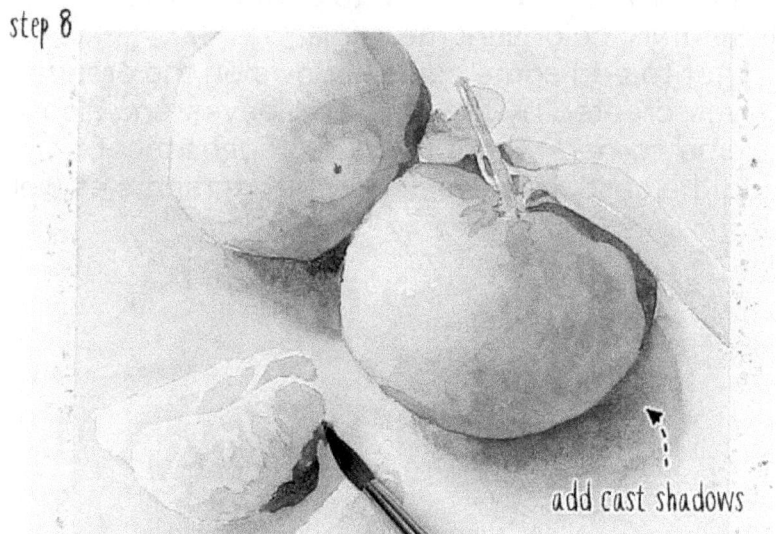

The final step is to add some details to the leaf using a darker toned green mixture. Leave gaps to let the underlying color show through, and to represent the veined texture on the leaves.

Still life is an excellent way to practice watercolors regularly with a high level of control over your choice of subject and composition setup.

And next time you have some oranges lying around, why not try this kind of painting for yourself!

Watercolor Still Life

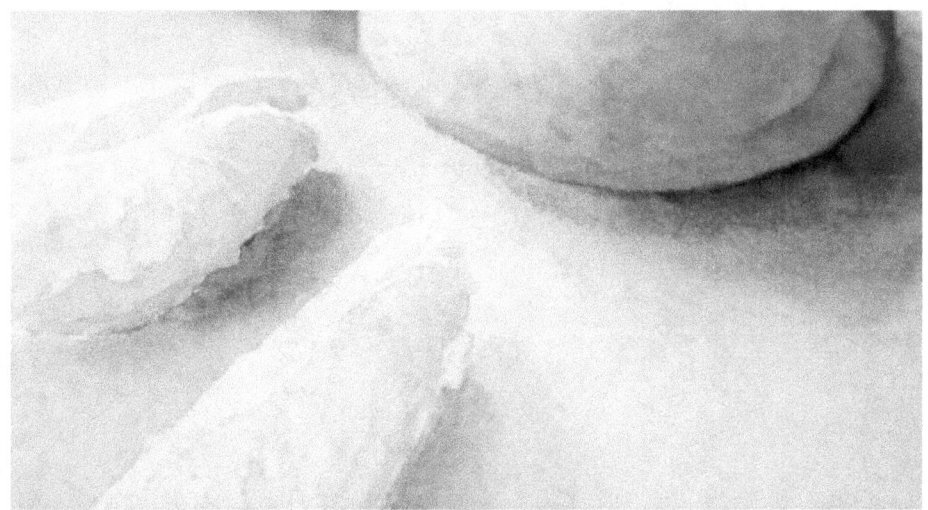

Did you ever wonder where the tradition of giving oranges at Christmas comes from?
Well... There are a few different versions, but one of the stories I seem to remember talks about how an orange represents the Christmas season of giving and sharing. This is because oranges can be split into segments and shared with others!
So, while I can't actually share a real orange with everybody, I can at least share this watercolor painting of an orange. *(actually this is a clementine, but shhh... just keep that to yourself, will you?)*

Watercolor Still Life

The advantages of still life in watercolor are considerable. However, what most artists love about still-life paintings is the amount of control they have.

Your subject can be arranged, lit, and set up in any way you like. You can move things around, change

Watercolor Coffee Painting

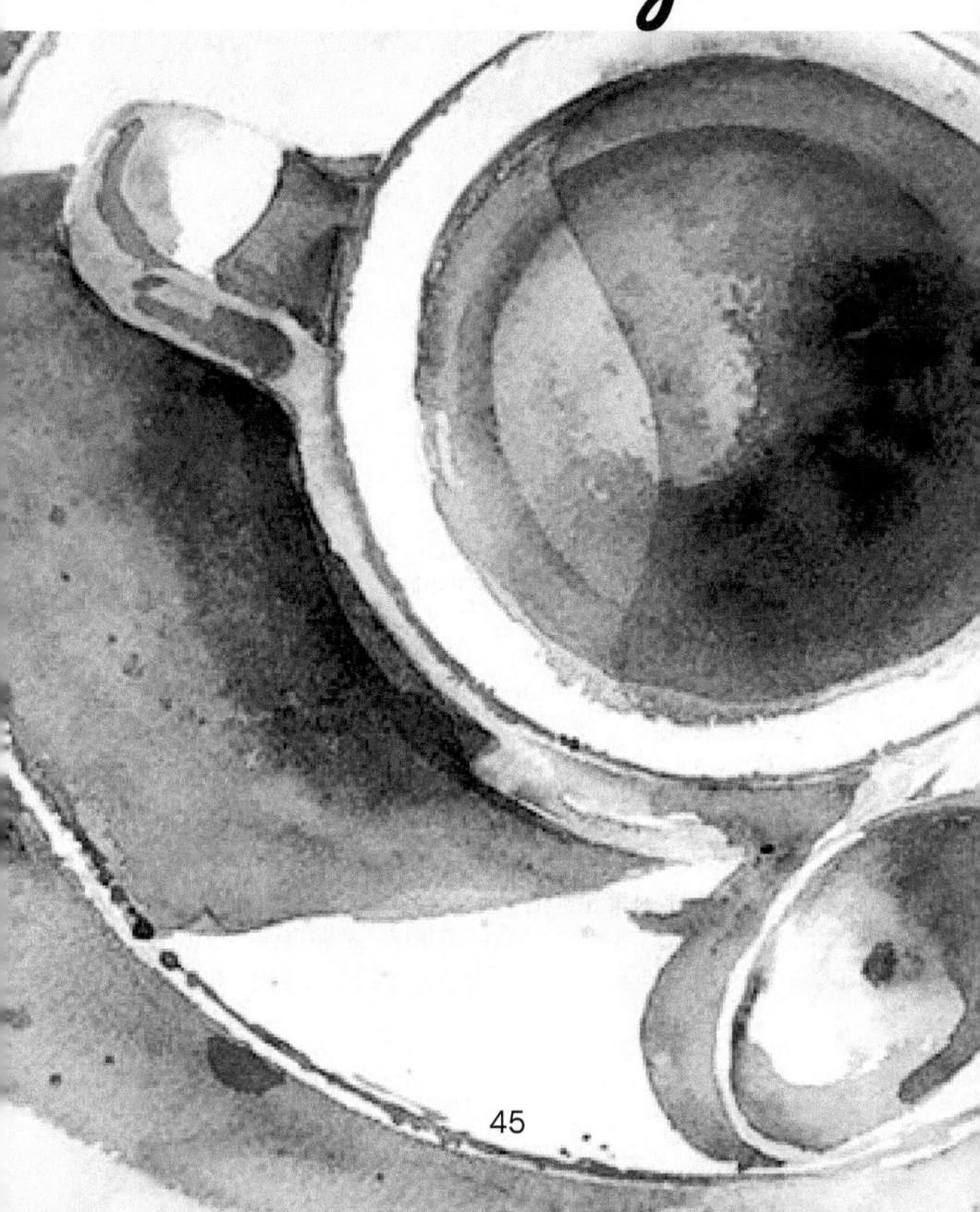

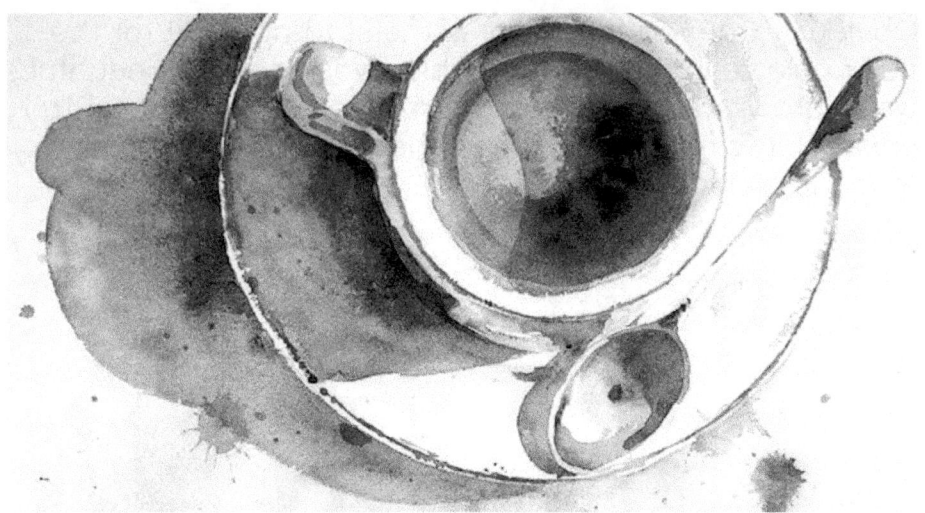

I've heard it said that coffee boosts creativity. Whether that's true or not, I thought you might like to join me by following along with this watercolor coffee cup tutorial. I'm always on the lookout for new subjects to paint. The ring stain of coffee on my desktop provided the inspiration for this latest watercolor. I was sipping my coffee this morning and putting the cup on a sheet of paper. This left a circular mark each time I put down the cup.

Messy me...

And this watercolor painting will include some messy texture effects. I wanted to add some drips and stains as a way of representing the fluid nature of the subject. Everybody needs a coffee break from time to time. So grab yourself a cup and give this painting a try. *(Just don't mistake your coffee for your rinse water!)*

Watercolor Coffee Cup – Colors, Composition and Style

Colors

Obviously, the "coffee" color is the starting point for the color palette in this painting. This gives us some beautiful warm browns and oranges. But rather than using a neutral grey color for the shading and shadows, I've tended towards a blue gray color.

I love this combination of hues. **A mix of oranges and blues like this produces a complementary color scheme.**

> Complementary colors are those which are opposite each other on the color wheel. This type of color scheme is highly contrasting and tends to produce interesting, vibrant results.

Composition

For the composition I chose an overhead view. I used a simple rule of thirds to position the center of the coffee cup in the overall composition.

> Using the rule of thirds, you simply divide the page into thirds with imaginary lines. Putting the subject along one of these intersecting lines creates a focal point for the coffee cup, and sets up a more dynamic composition. It's been shown that the human eye is more readily drawn to these dividing lines.

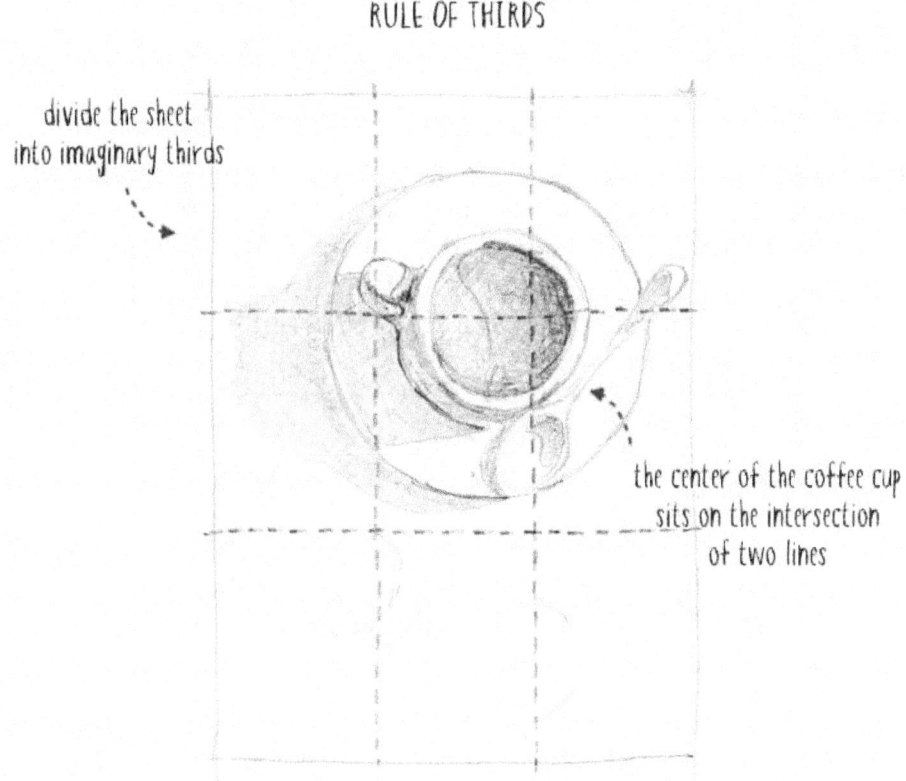

RULE OF THIRDS

divide the sheet into imaginary thirds

the center of the coffee cup sits on the intersection of two lines

Remember, where you leave space around your subject is almost as important as the subject itself.

Style

I was aiming for a loose watercolor painting style for this painting. To achieve this I used various techniques to add drips, splatters, and movement within the watercolors.

Watercolors are a medium which lend themselves well to loose painting techniques. Personally, I also find this a good exercise for learning to "let go", and not get too caught up in the details. That was one of my big problems when I started out as an artist.

Watercolor Coffee Cup Step by Step

I wasn't sure that I got off to a good start with this painting. But I kept going and things seemed to work out better.

This is something we all face from time to time with a new painting. I had an image in my mind of what I wanted to paint but the first few brushstrokes went amiss! The most important lesson here is "don't give up too soon". Persistence usually pays off, even if you find your watercolors don't look good in the early stages.

My approach was to work from the center of the painting outwards.

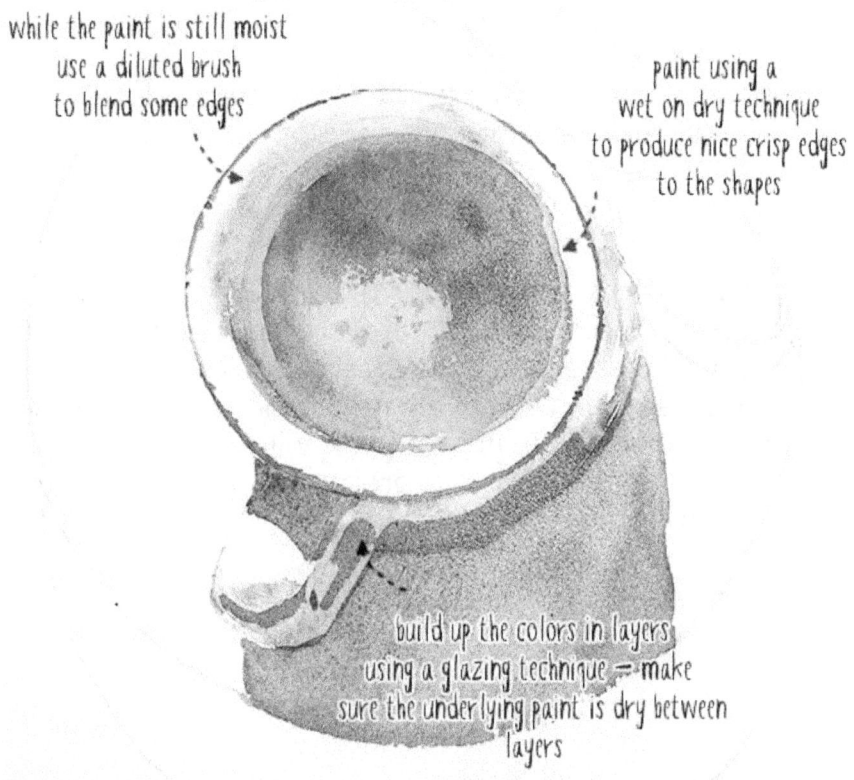

Step 1

WATERCOLOR COFFEE CUP TUTORIAL

while the paint is still moist use a diluted brush to blend some edges

paint using a wet on dry technique to produce nice crisp edges to the shapes

build up the colors in layers using a glazing technique – make sure the underlying paint is dry between layers

Step 1:
Begin by defining the cup in middle. To do this I used a watercolor technique known as wet on dry, but also some blending to smooth certain edges.
Different colors were laid on top of each other after the underlying paint was dry – in watercolors this produces an effect known as glazing.
By painting wet on dry (using a wet brush on dry paper) you can see that the shapes have sharp, well defined edges. This is true for most of the initial shape, with the exception of the upper lip where the color is blended, fading from a darker to a lighter hue.

To produce this blending effect you start by applying a brush stroke of strong color, then dip your brush in water, remove some of the excess moisture from the brush using a cloth or a sponge, then apply a new brush stroke to the edge of the first shape.
Repeat the process again, removing some more paint from your brush tip, then blotting the brush, before blending the shape some more.
By pulling the color outwards with the damp, diluted brush, you obtain a smooth gradient of color from dark to light.

The reason why you blot your brush to remove moisture is because you don't want your new brush stroke to be wetter than the wash of color on the paper. Remember, water will move from wet to dry. If your new brushstroke is too wet it will flood the initial color with diluted paint and probably cause what's known as a backwash or bloom.

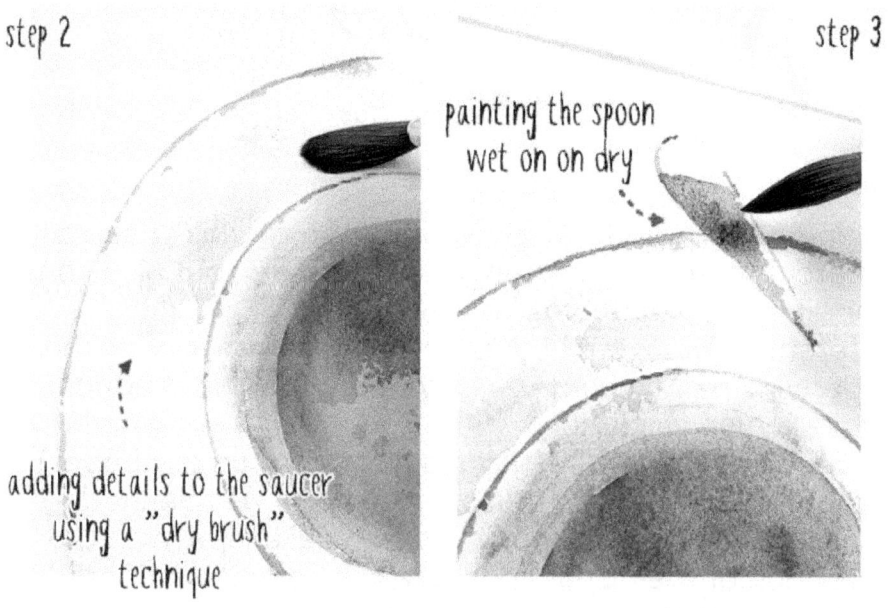

step 2

step 3

painting the spoon wet on on dry

adding details to the saucer using a "dry brush" technique

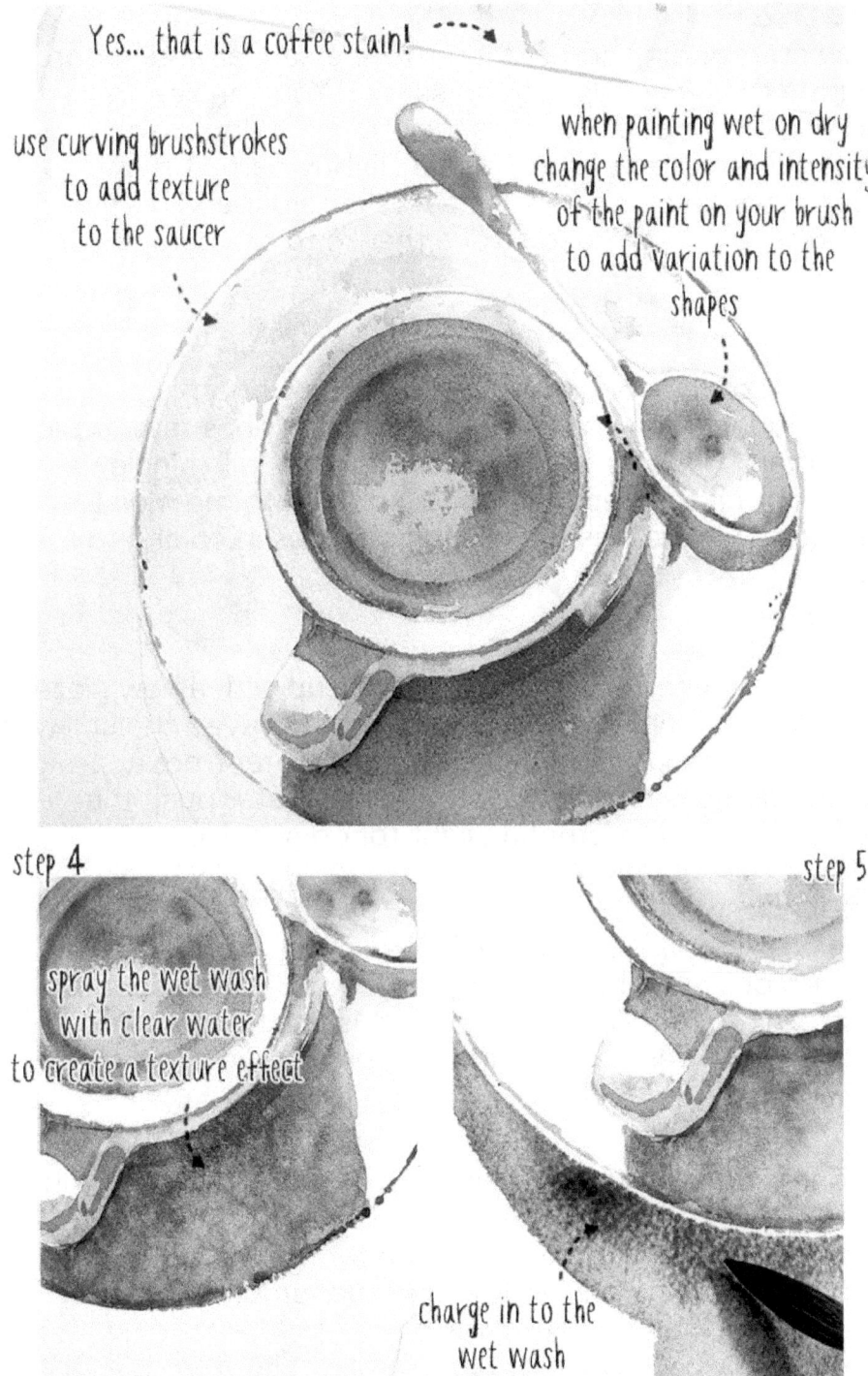

Step 2:
Now start adding some details to the saucer and spoon. Paint a thin dark edge to the saucer. You can see I'm adding a light color to the saucer using a drybrush technique. To do this you use a slightly damp brush and drag the side of the bristles across the paper. This gives a broken, textured brush stroke thanks to the bumpiness of the paper.

Step 3:
The rest of the spoon is painted with a wet on dry technique. When you paint like this, don't hesitate to pick up different colors with your brush. They will mingle together on the paper when you paint into the moist shapes. This creates interesting changes in color and value.

Step 4:
Next I deepened the shadow of the cup with a new glaze of blue gray paint. For added texture I sprayed the still wet wash of the shadow with a spatter of water from a "spritzer" bottle. The droplets of clear water push the damp paint aside, creating light toned speckles.

Step 5:
The next step is to add the final shadows. I painted with a wet on dry technique and added deeper toned shadows to the edge of the saucer. To do this I just charge into the already wet wash of the shadow shape.

> Charging in is a term in watercolor painting where you add more color to a damp wash. This is a way of mixing colors directly on the paper rather than in your palette. The colors will mix together smoothly and intensify the underlying wash.

step 6

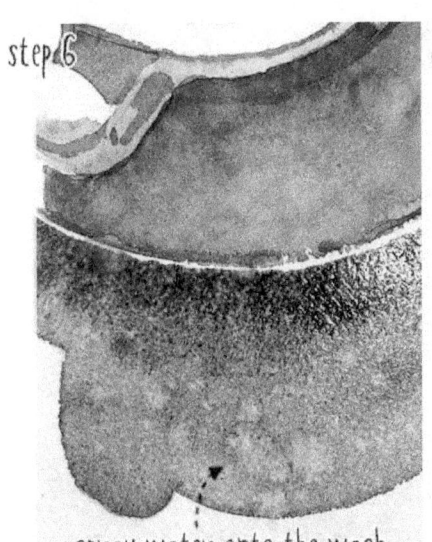

spray water onto the wash to create texture

step 7

deepen the coffee color by adding a dark blended shape

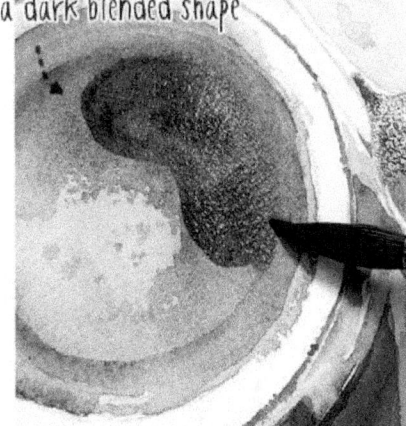

step 8

the finished cup & saucer

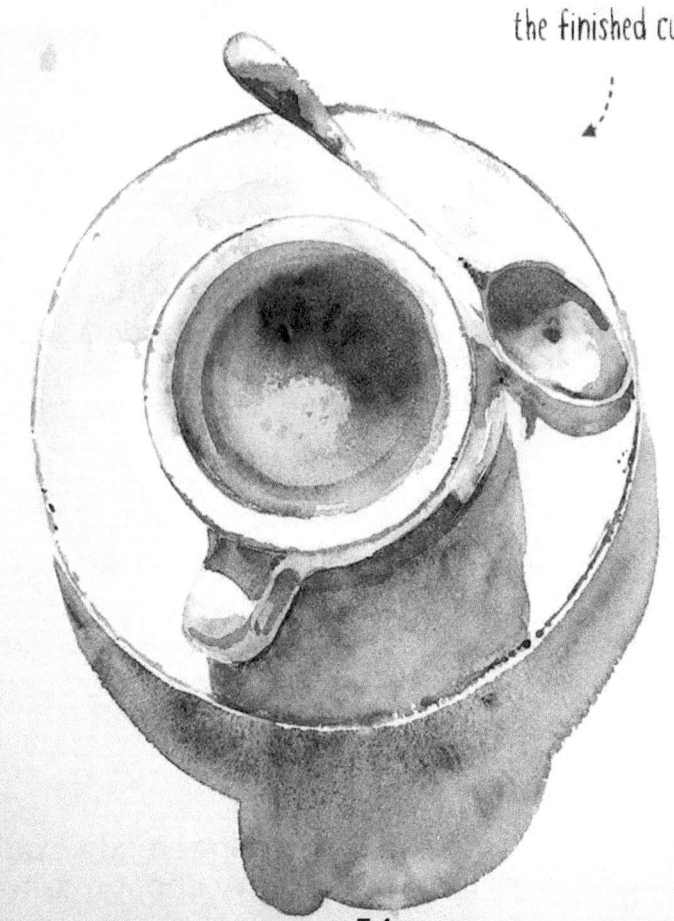

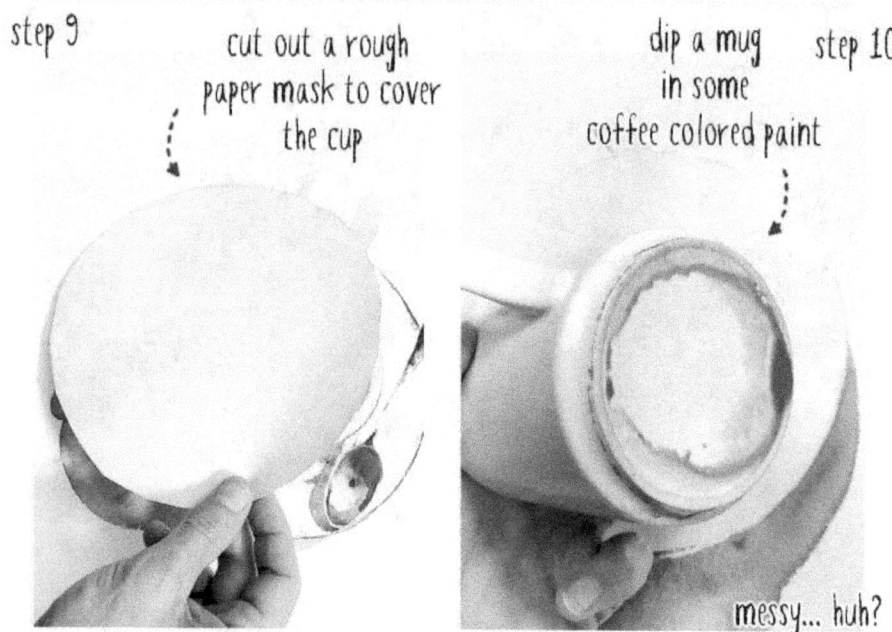

Step 6:
When the paint dries, add another glaze to the saucer shadows, then use a spray bottle again to add some texture with droplets of water.

Step 7:
At this stage I thought the coffee color needed deepening, so I added a dark shape of rich brown color (Burnt Umber). The edges of this shape were blended using the technique described above.

Step 8:
At this stage the cup and saucer are finished. But the fun isn't over yet! In the next stages we're working going to work on the background and add some liquid splatters and stains. This adds some visual interest to the overall painting.

Step 9:
To protect the finished cup from staining I made a quick paper cutout to cover it up. Don't worry about making an

accurate mask or using masking fluid. The loose nature of the painting means it doesn't matter if some of the paint flows back onto the cup.

Step 10:
To imitate the ringed coffee stains I got an old mug and dipped the bottom in some coffee colored paint. Use the mug like an ink stamp to print ring stains onto the paper.

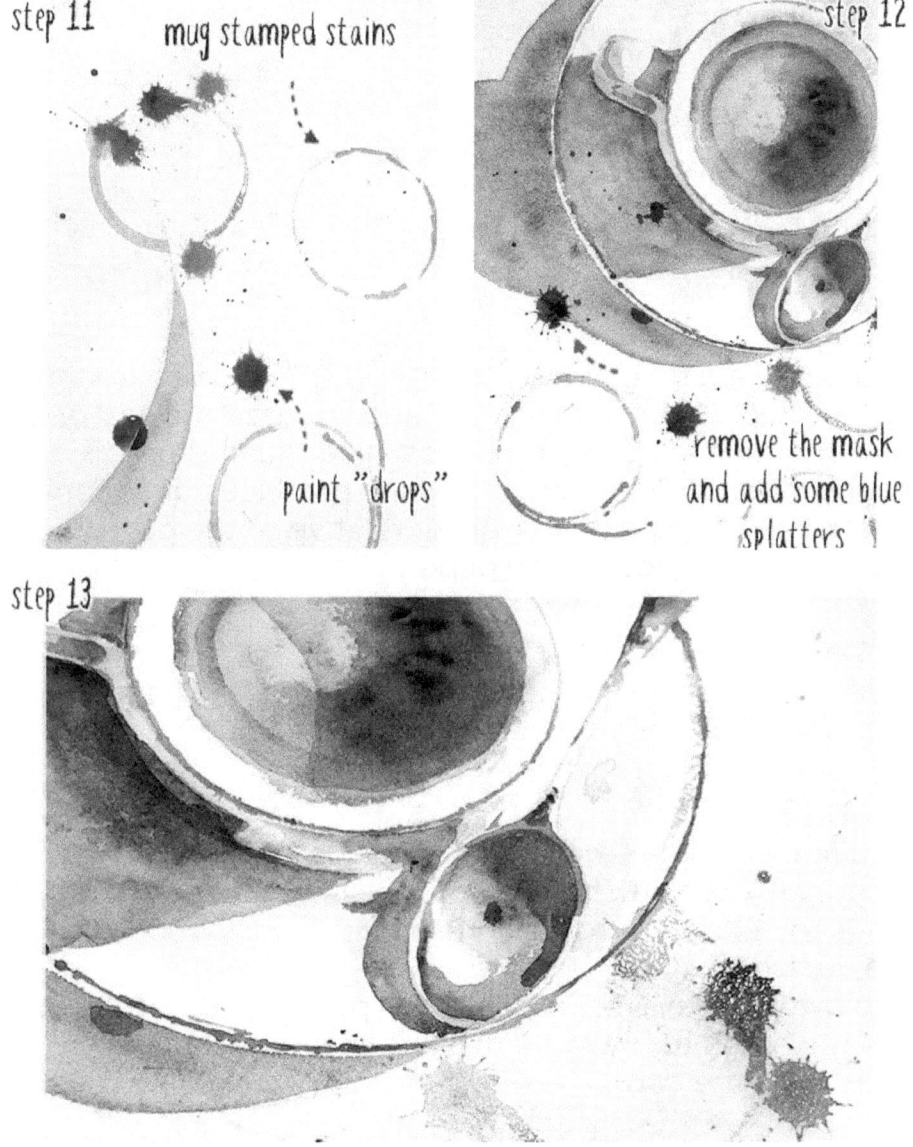

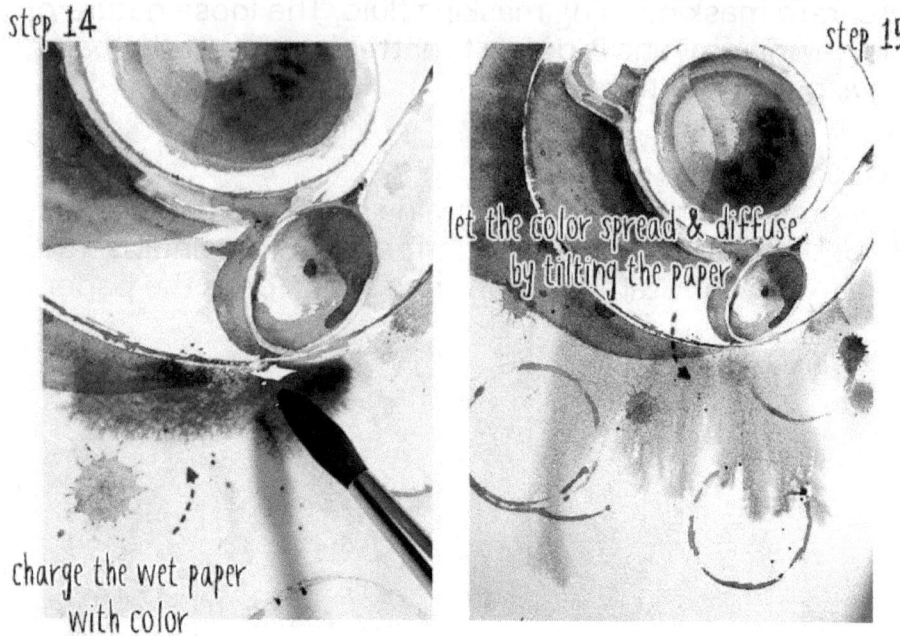

step 14 — charge the wet paper with color

step 15 — let the color spread & diffuse by tilting the paper

Step 11:
At the same time I added some drops of color. To do this, simply hold the brush vertically and squeeze the end of a soaked brush tip. This produces a nice round drop (as opposed to flicking the brush which produces directional splatters). The higher your brush relative to the page, the more it will explode on the paper.

Step 12:
Remove the paper mask from the cup and add some more drops and splatters, this time using a blue hue.

Step 13:
As a final touch for the background I used a wet on wet technique (wet brush onto wet paper) to add some diffused color. I started by brushing the background (not the cup shape) with clear water.
Don't worry if this makes the other paint marks run. Simply use the brush to blend them using linear brushstrokes away from the cup.

Step 14:
Load your brush with plenty of watercolor and use a charging in technique to apply color to the edge of the saucer. The paint will start to diffuse into the wet paper.

Step 15:
Let the color run away from the cup by tilting the paper.

Step 16:
Use a large brush and clear water to even out the diffused paint as necessary. The result should be a range of light colored soft shapes over the background.

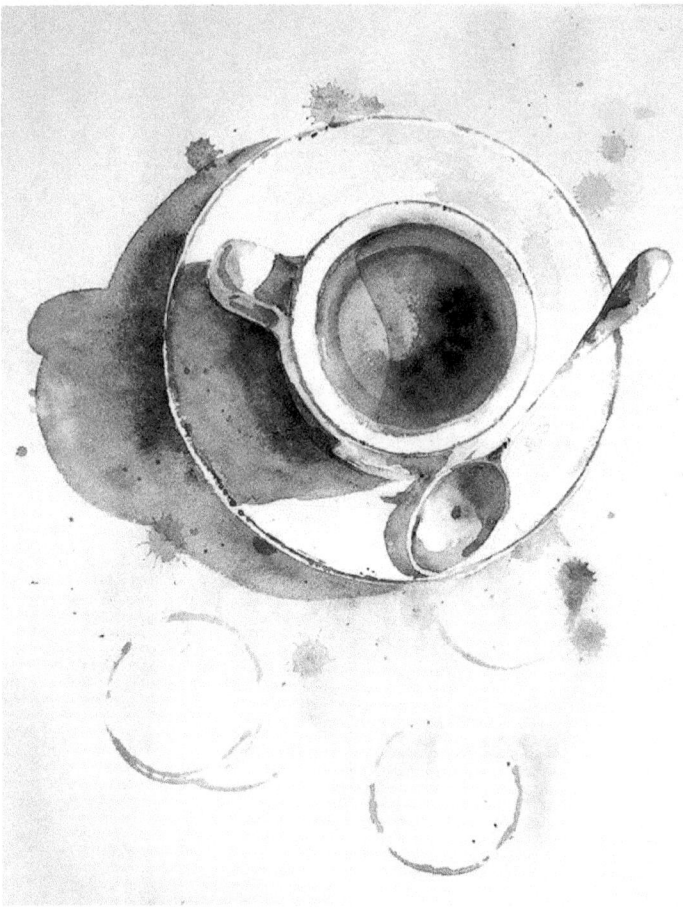

Your coffee cup watercolor painting is now complete. Pat yourself on the back and go show off to your friends!

How to Paint Watercolor Roses

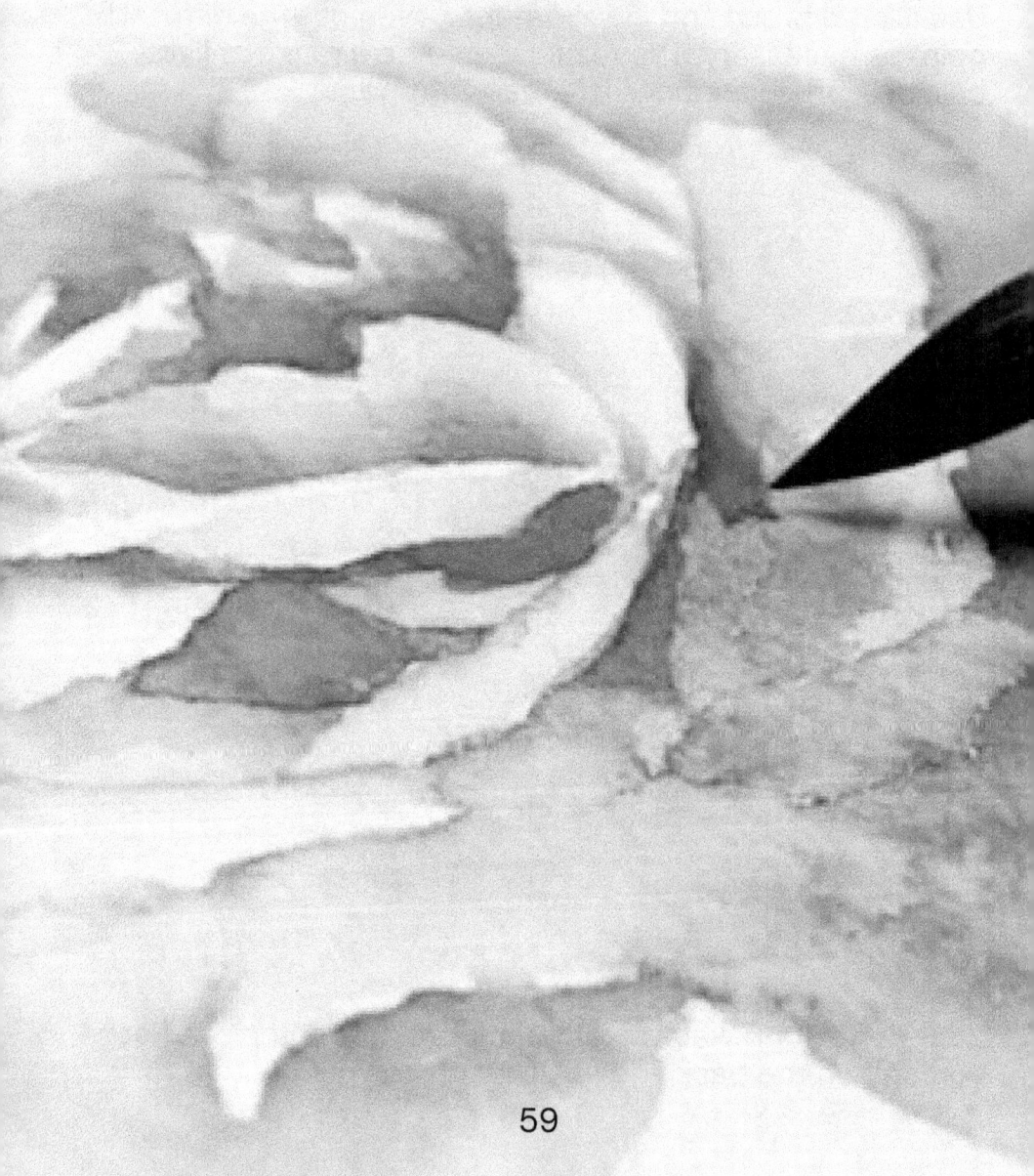

It's that time of year again.
(For those of you who've forgotten, I'm talking about Valentines day!)
And I know what a bunch of romantic folks you are, so in this step by step tutorial I'm going to show you how to paint a rose in watercolor. I'll go over all the details so you can understand the process from beginning to end.
What better way to paint this weekend ?!
Flowers are a favorite subject for a lot of artists but the forms of roses are particularly complicated, which can sometimes make painting these flowers a challenge.
If you want you can follow along and paint your own version of this composition. All the reference material and the sketch template can be downloaded below.
And who knows, you could end up with the perfect valentines gift *(psst... if you forgot to order flowers, all is not lost!)*

How to Paint Roses in Watercolor

Roses are fairly complex looking flowers which can make them seem difficult to paint.
The sketches below simplify the anatomy of a rose into basic geometric shapes. Understanding the structure like this will help us to figure out how it interacts with light and shadow.

The overall form of a rose can be compared to a cup.

The center of this cup contains a series of smaller closely packed petals that make up the inside of the rose.
The outside of the cup is surrounded by bigger petals which progressively curve outwards and unfold.

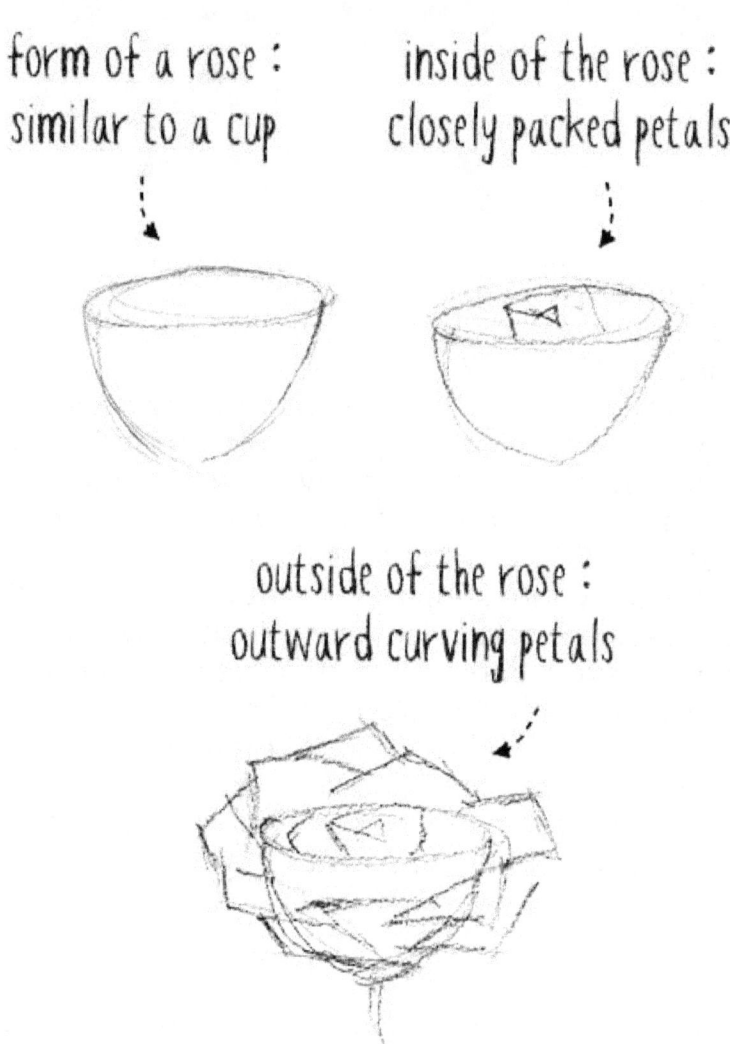

When you draw these three basic elements you start to get something which resembles a rose.

As a general rule when a rose is lit from above, the upper part of the rose will appear lighter than the bottom part.

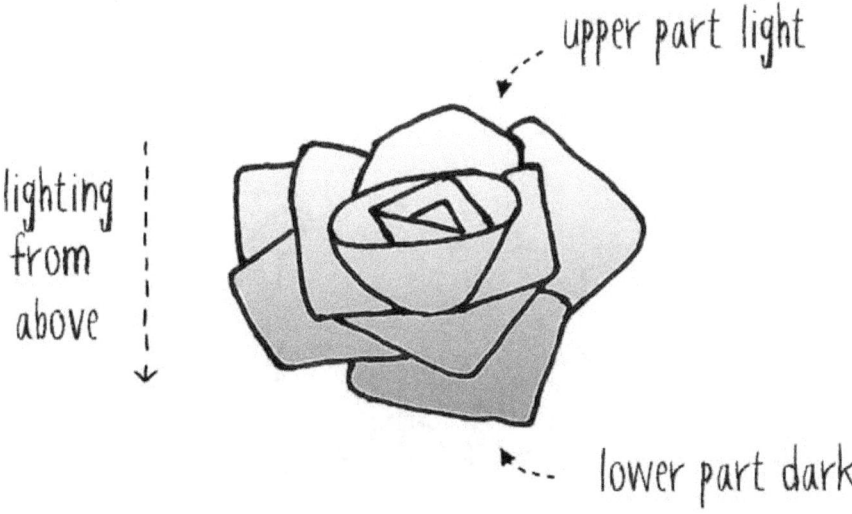

Also, because of the way the petals converge towards the center of the rose, each petal will look lighter at the tip and get progressively darker as it reaches the heart of the flower.

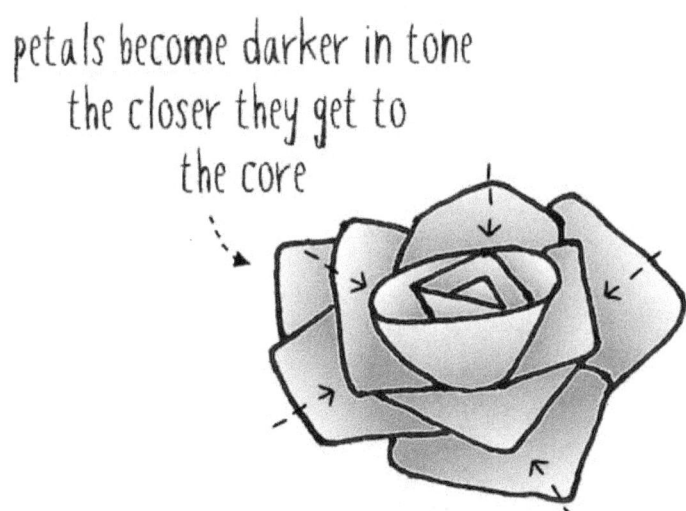

The combined effect is that the tonal values of a rose get progressively darker from top to bottom (light at the top and dark at the base), and from the tips of the petals towards the center as they gradually become hidden from the light.

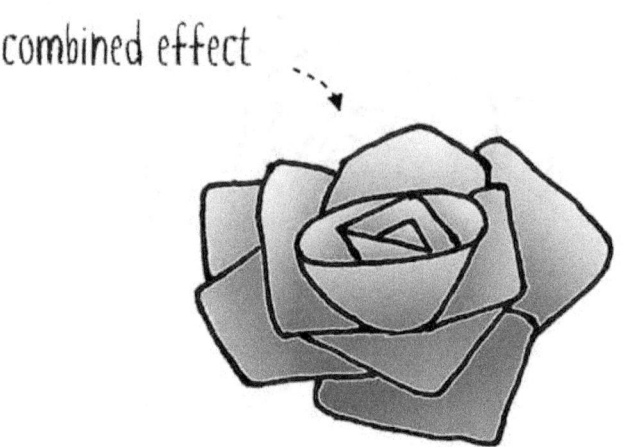

Simply keeping these ideas in mind about how the light and shading changes across the surface of the flower is enough to be able to paint a reasonable interpretation of a watercolor rose without even trying to copy the subject exactly.

Watercolor Rose Sketch

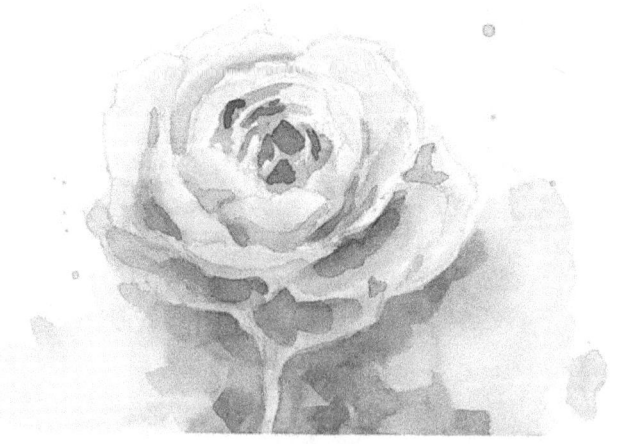

Before tackling the final painting I did a quick watercolor rendering, following the "tonal value rules" we just described.

First I sketched a freehand version of a rose which approximates the geometry of the flower, with tightly spaced petals in the center and larger unfolding petals on the outside.

The idea is to do a loose painting as a warm up for the final watercolor, so I'm not trying to be very accurate with my brush strokes and at the same time I can test out my paint mixtures.

I begin with a very light and diluted pink color, charged with some yellow for a bit of variety.

I paint the petal shapes, keeping in mind the overall rules for shading. You can see that I try to leave some white highlights for the tips of the petals where they would be the most exposed to light. And I make the inner folds of the petals darker because these are the parts which are the most shaded.

I use a glazing technique to add more layers of paint to strengthen the values of the underside of the rose which would logically be more shaded. And I leave the petals at the top and on the outer edges light in color. A single layer of diluted paint is enough for these shapes.

As a final touch I add a few brush marks of darker paint to the most shaded parts of the flower, such as the folds on the lowest petals, and the core of the rose which is generally quite dark because of the concentration of closely spaced petals in the center.

I'm not really worried about blending edges at this stage. I just want the overall tonal values to look approximately right.

I added a quick background using a contrasting green color to help the flower stand out on the page.

I find it can be useful to do a loose watercolor sketch like this before you commit to the final painting. It's a good way to familiarize yourself with a subject.

Watercolor Rose Step by Step

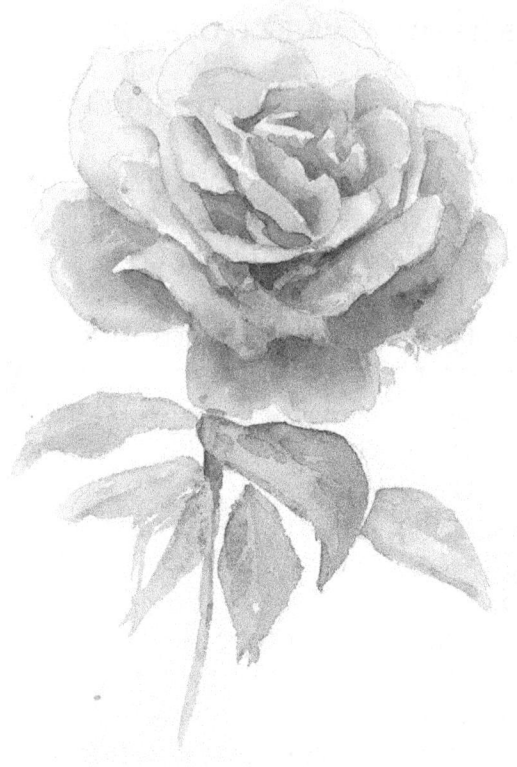

Here are the paint colors I used :

- Quinacridone rose – Pigment number: PV19

- Pyrrol scarlet – Pigment number: PR255

- Hansa Yellow Deep – Pigment number: PY65

- Phthalo Green BS – Pigment number: PG7

- French Ultramarine – Pigment number: PB29

This is the reference photo I chose for my final rose painting.

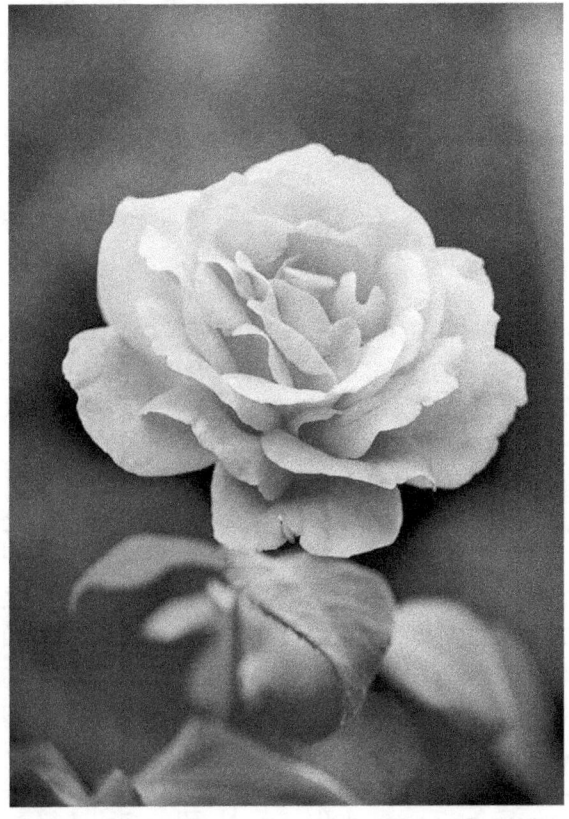

Begin by transferring the outline of the rose onto a sheet of watercolor paper and tape it down to a flat board using masking tape.
I begin painting the flower from the center outwards using a medium strength mixture of quinacridone rose. (You'll find a list of all the colors I used for this painting below).
I applied my first brush marks to the inner folds of the petals where they are darkest in tone, then using a rinsed and blotted brush, I blended the color outwards to become lighter at the tips. You can use the reference photo as a guide to help you with this.
Keep working from the middle outwards using the same method. You can also charge in some different colors such as warmer reds or yellows to add some color variation.

When you reach the outer petals towards the bottom you should adjust your paint mixture so the petals appear shaded. To do this added a small amount of french ultramarine to make a purple-violet color.
In the real world, outdoor lighting tends to be warm, which produces shadows with a cool blue-violet appearance. The result will be much more colorful and realistic than if you try to use a dark colored paint such as gray or brown. Brown is too warm and will produce the wrong color for shading and shadows in this situation.

Continue painting the outer petals at the top of the flower, but of course this time you need to use a diluted light-toned pink color. As you can see in the reference photo the very top of the rose is brightly lit.
As you progress downwards, you can use stronger colored paint. I'm working using mostly a wet-on-dry technique. I apply brush marks directly onto the dry paper, then I rinse my brush and blend out the edges to get a smooth gradient of color from dark to light. Just make sure your brush isn't too wet when you start blending, or you might flood the existing wash and cause unwanted stains known as "blooms".
I use stronger colors as I reach the bottom of the flower, and I also drop in some additional color in places where the paper is still wet. This is a wet-on-wet technique known as "charging-in".

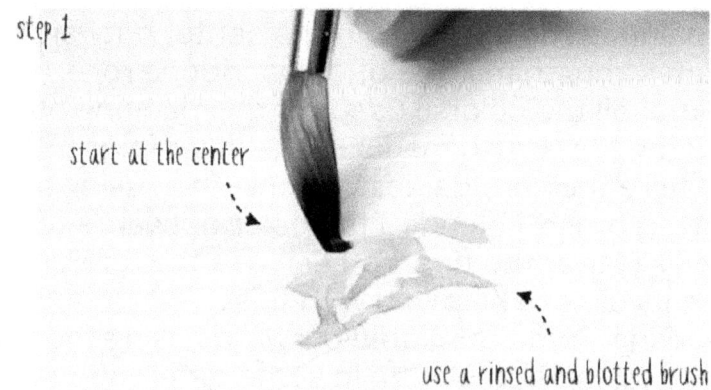

step 1

start at the center

use a rinsed and blotted brush
to blend out the edges

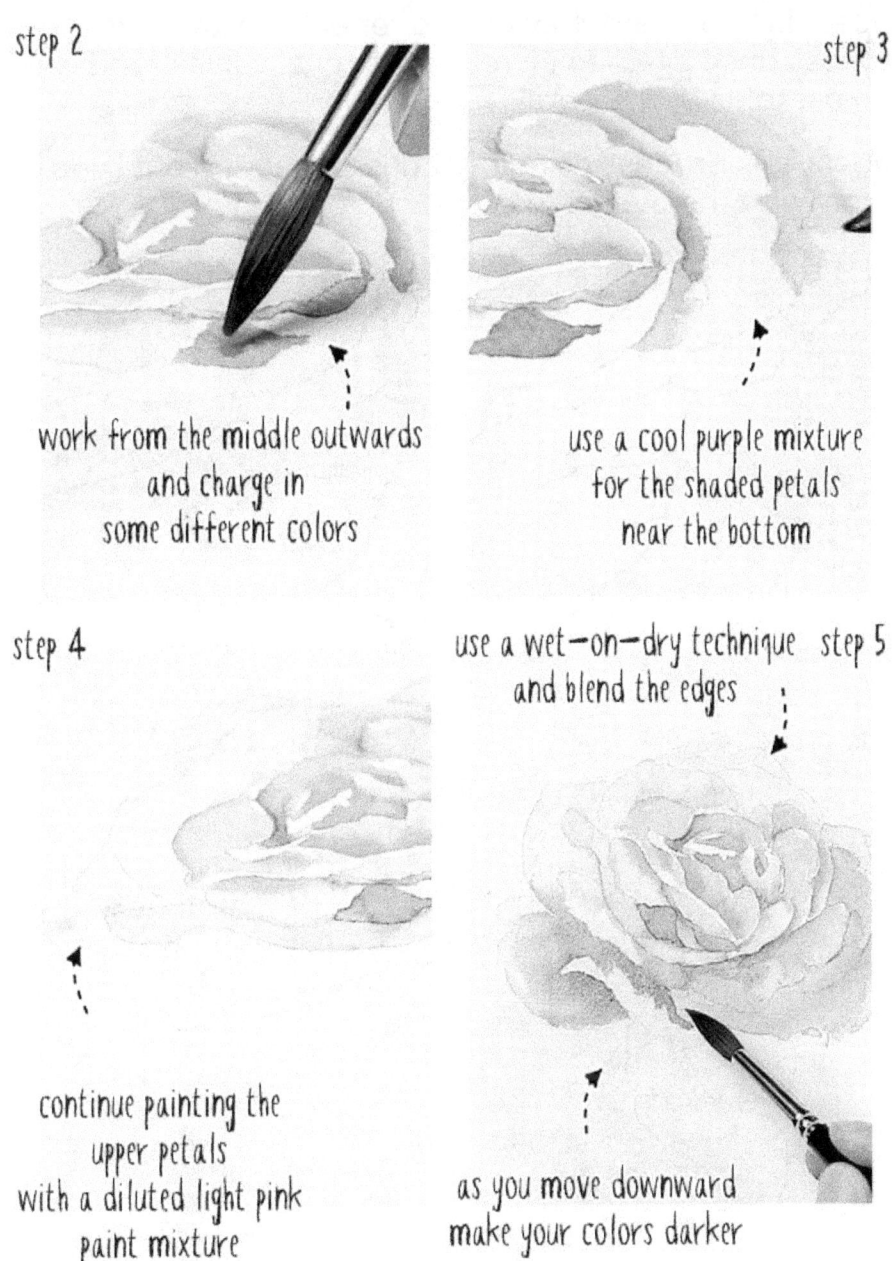

step 2

work from the middle outwards and charge in some different colors

step 3

use a cool purple mixture for the shaded petals near the bottom

step 4

continue painting the upper petals with a diluted light pink paint mixture

step 5

use a wet-on-dry technique and blend the edges

as you move downward make your colors darker

Let the paint dry then go back over the parts that need stronger values such as the center of the flower and the petals on the underside which are in shadow.
Leave the paint to dry again. You'll find that watercolors

appear lighter when they dry, so repeat the layering process once again to increase the tonal values for the darkest folds of the petals.

Repeat this process as many times as needed until you're happy with the overall result.

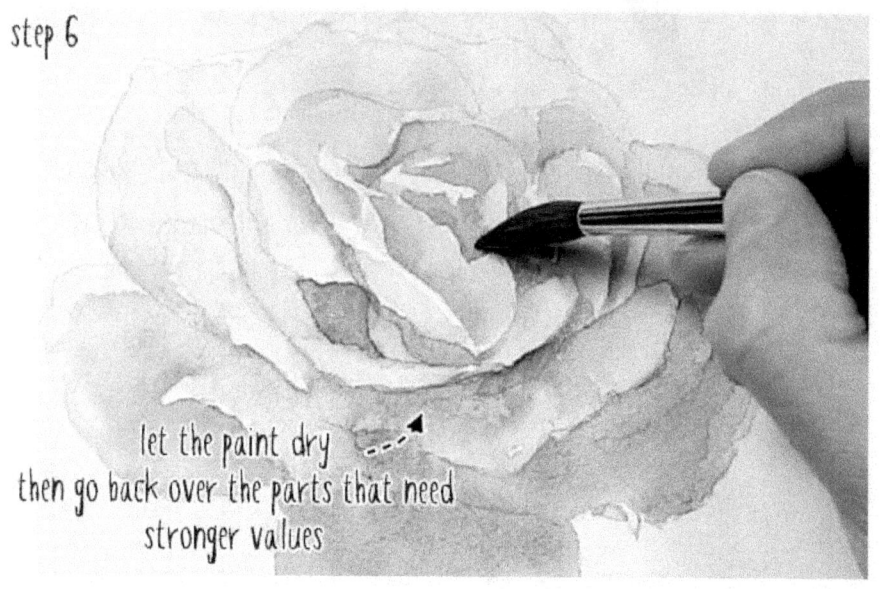

step 6

let the paint dry then go back over the parts that need stronger values

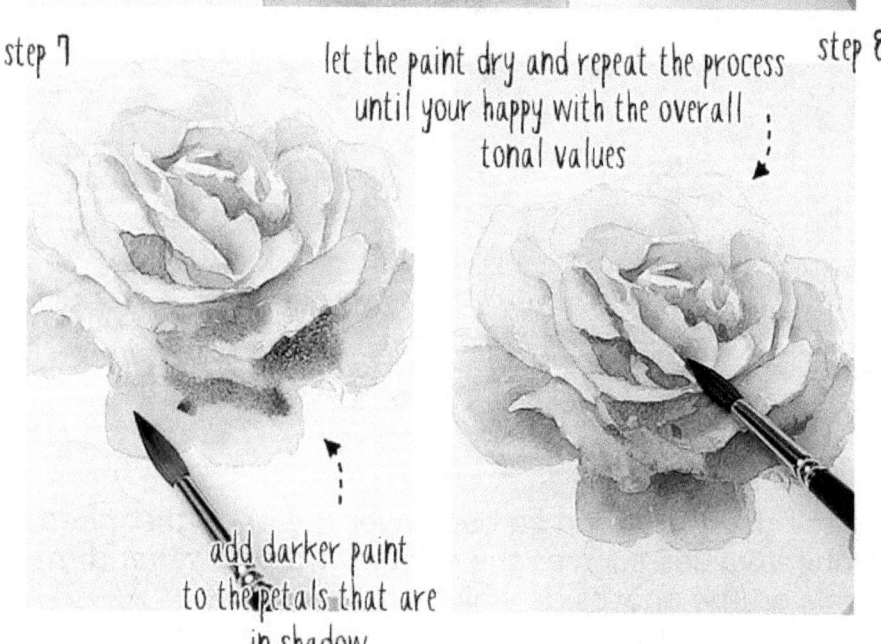

step 7

add darker paint to the petals that are in shadow

let the paint dry and repeat the process until your happy with the overall tonal values

step 8

Now that the flower is complete you can move on to the leaves and the stem.

I painted these in a very loose style. I didn't want to add too much detail to the leaves because these are not the main focus of the painting.
I paint these using quick brush strokes without trying to be too accurate. While the shapes are still wet I take advantage to either drop in different colored greens or use a dried brush to blot up the paint. The objective is to create loose leaf shapes with variation in tone and color. When the first layer of paint is dry I added a few quick brush strokes to add some texture to the leaves. Nothing too precise, just a suggestion of the kind of patterns you find on leaves.
And here's the finished painting...

Thank for reading

www.ingramcontent.com/pod-product-compliance
Lightning Source LLC
Chambersburg PA
CBHW050238230526
45470CB00005B/2008